Psalm 57:1-3

No More Fear

40 days to conquer worry

JoHannah Reardon

DEDICATION

To my husband, Brad, who has helped me to love God and his Word, and to find my refuge in Jesus Christ alone.

My Battle with Fear

Ten years ago, if you had asked me if I was a worrier, I would have said no. I thought I took most things in stride and was able to put things in perspective. However, when my mother died, I began having panic attacks now and then, jarring me into realizing that perhaps I was feeling more anxious than I thought.

Amy Simpson, in her book *Anxious*, says she lived with such a high level of anxiety for so long that she didn't even recognize it and thought it was normal. I began to slowly realize that I might have a similar problem. I began to have a creeping thought that underlying my daily life was a huge amount of anxiety, but I was too busy and unwilling to face it. Besides, I didn't know what to do about it if I did admit it head on.

All of that changed a few years ago. I am not part of a church that regularly practices Lent, but I work with people who do. Their mentioning it often enough made me stop and think about the practice, and as I did I felt it would be good for me to give up something for 40 days, helping me to see my addictions and dependencies. In our indulgent, instant-gratification society, I saw the value of voluntarily depriving myself of something in order to focus more on who God is and how much I need him.

When I first started practicing Lent, I followed everyone else's suggestions and gave up a certain food or media. Those experiences were fairly useful in revealing deep-seated habits, and thus made me more aware of my need for my Savior. But several years ago, I took time to pray about what I should give up. I asked God to show me a dependency that truly was hindering my relationship with him.

I thought about foods, but I'm a fairly disciplined eater, so that didn't seem to be a problem area for me. I'm also not a big media junky, so I didn't feel compelled to go that route again. As I continued to ponder it before God, I had the strong impression that I was to give up worry for 40 days.

When I told my husband my decision, he looked at me skeptically. "Aren't you supposed to give up something you enjoy for Lent?" He had a good point, but since I wasn't tied to any church tradition anyway, I felt I could practice Lent any way I wanted. And once the idea of giving up worry for 40 days began to take hold, I felt more and more strongly that this was the course for me.

Again, the funny thing was that if you'd asked me if I was a worrier, I would have said no, even as I felt compelled to give up worry. I have a pretty *laissez faire* attitude toward life—at least that's what I've always told myself. I've usually faced the big things in life with trust rather than panic. So I could understand my husband's attitude about me giving up worry. What's the big deal about that? But I felt the nudge as strongly as I've felt anything, so I went with it.

Although I sensed this conviction pretty strongly, nothing prepared me for the next 40 days, which turned out to be some of the most amazing, faith-filled days of my life. And to my surprise, I found out that worry has been one of my most deep-seated, tenacious sins.

My Fear of Violent Men Consumed Me

Although I faced the big things with courage and trust, I didn't realize I carried the burden of all the little things with constant fear and uncertainty. And many of them were wrapped up in fear of violent men.

I believe this began when I was a child and first was warned about Stranger Danger. Suddenly, I began to see everyone I didn't know as suspicious—particularly men. This was a problem, since my father owned a restaurant. Every day after school I went there, ate dinner, and stayed until my mother took me home at bedtime. And each time a man looked at me or tried to be friendly with me, I imagined he was evil and about to snatch me away from my family forever. As a result, I would eat my dinner and then go to my father's office and hide the rest of the time.

My parents thought I was shy, and I never told them the real reason I hid. If I had discussed it with them, I am sure they would have given me perspective and helped me through my irrational fear, but I didn't do that because I hadn't analyzed it well enough myself. I was only eight years old.

This fear of evil men grew as I did. In my teens, I began reading stories of women who were raped by strangers, and I remember seeing a movie about a man who stalked a woman for months so that he could take her unaware and attack her when she least expected it. This movie would haunt me for years. Wherever I went, I was suspicious that an evil man was watching me, waiting for such an opportunity.

As I look back on it now, I realize that my imagination was a big part of the problem. One of my favorite quotes is "Worry is a misuse of the imagination" (Dan Zadra). And as I've talked to others, I've realized that those who worry often do have good imaginations. We live in our thought lives enough that we can spin tales of horror very easily. When asked what he was afraid of, Stephen King said, "Everything!"

When I discussed my fear of evil men with my adult daughter, who lives fearlessly most of the time, she asked, "Have you ever actually met the kind of evil man you are envisioning?" I had to admit that I hadn't. It hit me like a slap on the face that I'd feared someone whom I was unlikely to ever meet. But evil men do stalk women and cause horrible things to happen to them. Evil men do give women date rape drugs, promise them anything to get sex, and abuse women in any way they can. However, I learned through 40 days of giving up worry that I didn't have to be consumed with the fear of those things happening.

For example, within the first week of giving up worry, I took a walk in a park near our house. As I was walking along the path, I came to a section that followed a road. Out of the corner of my eye, I noticed a man in a truck slowly keeping pace with me. Now, let me reassure you that this is a very safe park in a very safe community, and that there were other people around. Nevertheless, noticing something like this would usually have put me in an all-out panic, and I would have taken off running in the opposite direction. All my natural instincts were screaming at me to do this. But the first thing that came to mind was, *I gave up worry for Lent. I do not need to worry about this.* My body began to relax. While I was still aware and certainly not trying to be naïve, I refused to allow the worry of what-if to consume me and take away the joy of my walk. When I turned the corner, the truck went on. I realized in that moment that my almost daily fears of men were mostly unfounded.

Later on during Lent, my husband left on a two-week mission trip. Being alone in my house at night has been a long-time, deep-seated source of terror for me. For years, whenever my husband left overnight, I'd double check that all the doors and windows were locked and even stacked things against the door at night. I never wanted to go to bed when he was gone, so I'd stay up much later than normal and watch mindless TV or surf the computer until the wee hours so I didn't have to turn out all the lights and go to sleep. I'd finally drop off to sleep when I simply couldn't stay awake any longer. I knew this wasn't healthy, but I simply didn't know how to get over it.

This time, when the anxiety began to build toward evening, I recalled that I'd given up worry. I put my night in God's hands and refused to think about it any more. I locked my doors and didn't give them another thought. I went to bed at my normal time and slept soundly. I cannot describe the victory I felt. I realized I'd been trapped in a ridiculous web of fear for years. That lifetime habit of worry and terror was broken in one night, and it hasn't returned. Although I'd tried giving this fear over to God before, until I identified it as a deep-seated sin of worry and took 40 days to break free from it, I wasn't able to find relief.

I Really Can Trust God

In hindsight, I can see that giving up worry for those 40 days was Holy Spirit–inspired. There were so many little things that would have driven me crazy. For example, my husband and I went to London to celebrate a milestone anniversary. While there, we took a ferry from London to a tourist site. After we arrived, we decided we wanted to see two different things, so we agreed to meet at a little outdoor café we'd passed as we came in.

Within about twenty minutes, I lost interest in the attraction I'd gone to see and decided to head back to the café—but it wasn't there. I was sure it was in a certain direction, but I couldn't find it anywhere. I began to stop passersby to ask if they knew of an outdoor café with orange umbrellas. No one did.

The panic was rising, compounded by the fact that our phones didn't work in England so we had no way of contacting each other. Finally, I remembered I'd given up worry, and prayed, *Lord, you know where this café is. I trust you to show me.* I relaxed and noticed a group of college students singing Christian songs across the street. I meandered over and listened to them awhile. As they sang, all residual panic washed away. I began looking around and saw orange umbrellas in the distance.

I would never have seen them if I hadn't stopped to listen to the students sing. And I would never have relaxed enough to listen to them sing if I hadn't given up my panic. Most of all, I basked in the realization that God had known those college students would be on the corner just when I needed them.

From London, my husband flew to Africa for his mission trip. Normally, the two weeks he was there would have been excruciating for me. I would have worried about every little thing concerning his safety. His prayer requests would have increased my anxiety as I worried about each of those things as well. But when fears assaulted me during those two weeks, I let them drift away into God's hands. It was an amazingly relaxed and peaceful time.

Since then, my husband has joined a mission group, so he travels to Africa regularly. God in his kindness began preparing me for that during those 40 days. He knew I would need to trust him for my husband's safety.

For example, my husband was in Kenya when Somali militants killed 147 students at a Kenyan university. If this had happened before I took 40 days to give up worry, I would have lived in absolute terror until he got home. But instead, I placed him in God's hands and rested in God's goodness.

Worry Was My Thinly Veiled Attempt to Control My Circumstances

What my 40 days without worry also taught me is that I'm an overly responsible person. I try to be so responsible that I take on everyone else's worries too. I feel that if I can think my way through every difficulty and challenge, I'll be able to meet them with courage. I try to imagine everything that can go wrong so I can prevent those things from happening, and in the process, I take on the weight of the world that only God can handle. Since I've realized that, though, I've been able to consciously let it go and have felt amazing peace and relief.

When the 40 days were over, I didn't forget the lessons I'd learned. Many of the patterns and the reasons behind them are broken. I don't imagine that I'll ever have to face them as relentlessly as I did during that period of time.

Since then, I've told my story over and over. Many I've mentioned it to admit they have a problem with worry but were put off by the fact that I was talking about Lent. Because they, like me, were not raised with the tradition of Lent, the mention of it sounded legalistic and scared them off. Therefore, I am quick to tell people that giving up worry doesn't have to happen during Lent. It can be at any time of the year. The timing isn't important; what is important is that taking 40 days to break a habit is a sound principle.

So whether you practice Lent or not, this book will help you stay accountable as you give up your worries and fears. It provides a daily way to stay on track. And, even more importantly, it provides 40 days of looking at Scripture to see who God is. As we become firmly rooted in his perfect character, we learn to trust him. And as we learn to trust him, we unclench our fists and let go of our fears. Concentrating on letting them go for 40 days can break the stranglehold they have on you for good.

Facing Our Fears

If you are fearful and anxious, you may be able to mask it very well for years, as I did. In fact, you may mask it so well that you don't even recognize it as being a problem, but it will eventually catch up with you and affect your emotional, spiritual, and physical well being.

Once I recognized my own anxiety, I began to see it everywhere, in everyone. Interestingly, it has been easiest to see in the children I am around. As we mature, most of us learn to tamp down our anxiety so it's invisible to the world—and often to ourselves—but children have not yet learned that skill.

When I pointed out some poison ivy to my grandson, he was suddenly uncontrollably itchy all over, even though we were nowhere near it and he hadn't touched it. I thought this was ridiculous until I began thinking about how I often do the same thing. For example, when a friend of mine found out she had cancer, I began experiencing some of the symptoms she had, causing me all sorts of unnecessary fear. As Michel de Montaigne, an influential writer of the French Resistance, said, "He who fears he shall suffer, already suffers what he fears."

When my three-year-old granddaughter wouldn't go into my basement because there might be lions down there, I laughed at the ridiculousness of her irrational fear. But then I began thinking about all the times I'd imagined someone lurking in a dark alley waiting to spring at me. In a sense, our fears are not different at all.

I recently talked to a middle-school student who'd joined the track team. She loved the practices, but on days they had a meet, she would become so anxious she felt like throwing up. Her friends had similar reactions when they had to give a speech or take a standardized test. They all thought it was great to run with or chat with friends, but it was another thing to compete with them for a trophy or a grade.

As we get older, school fears are replaced with anxiety about our jobs. In today's fiercely competitive market, most of us fear not living up to expected standards, so we work longer and harder to try to prove ourselves. But the specter of fear is looming over us all the time.

We fear our future—that we won't be able to make ends meet or that we'll live inconsequential lives that won't amount to anything. We long to be noticed and affirmed, but fear we will always live in obscurity and meaninglessness. Like Solomon in Ecclesiastes, we fear coming to the end of our lives and saying, "Everything is meaningless . . . completely meaningless!" (Ecc. 1:2, NLT).

We fear loneliness—that we will never find someone to share our life with or who will understand our deepest needs and desires. Or perhaps we are stuck with someone who doesn't really comprehend who we are, so we feel alone, even though we are with a life partner. We find different ways to cope, but in our quiet moments of honesty, the fear of being alone is overwhelming.

On the flip side, we fear people. It's safer to keep relationships shallow, so we decide that getting involved with others is just not worth it. Instead, we get a pet and give it all our love and affection since animals can't hurt us the way humans do.

We fear standing for our faith, because we know doing so will have consequences. We'd like to be bolder, but we fear that we will be rejected, so we let opportunities to stand for Christ drift away until we don't even recognize them as opportunities anymore.

Nineteenth-century author Elizabeth Cady Stanton said, "The moment we begin to fear the opinions of others and hesitate to tell the truth that is in us . . . the divine floods of light and life no longer flow into our souls."

We face anxiety because of all the choices we have. In his book *The Concept of Anxiety*, Søren Kierkegaard said, "Anxiety is the dizziness of freedom." The more choices we are given, the more anxiety we feel. We love our privileges and freedoms, and yet they complicate our lives. The more choices we have, the more opportunities we have, and the more options we have, the more our anxiousness rises. Dizziness indeed!

Fear and worry are nothing new, but today our knowledge of all the bad that is happening in the world multiplies our anxiety exponentially. We have informational access to all the disasters of the world but are limited by time and space to do anything about them. We are bombarded daily with needs we can't meet and evil we can't comprehend.

We fear falling behind socially. As the trends change in fashion, pop culture, media, and language, it becomes harder and harder to stay relevant. We fear others will discount us because we haven't kept up. And in our youth-worshiping culture, we fear aging above all, which eventually backfires on all of us. A *Psychology Today* article titled "Learning to Love Growing Old" claims that the fear of aging speeds the very decline we dread most.

Fear dictates what we will try. We'd like to go for that job, date, adventure, (you fill in the blank), but stepping into the unknown means we might fail . . .

All these fears are multiplied when we start a family and become responsible for other tiny humans who seem so vulnerable and easily wounded. As parents, we can become frightened beyond all reason as we try to protect these fragile creatures given to our care. We fear our children will come to physical or emotional harm.

We fear we will ultimately not be good parents and will fail them. We fear they will wander from the faith or choose a lifestyle far from the one we want them to live. We fear the world they will inherit and the trials they will have to face. We fear they will make bad choices, choose the wrong friends, become bad people, marry the wrong person, pick the wrong job . . . in other words, we are afraid they will make many of the same mistakes we've made.

But in spite of all the valid reasons to worry, it's a problem when we take on those anxieties as our own and carry their weight. As Steve Maraboli says in *Life, the Truth, and Being Free*, "Your fear is 100% dependent on you for its survival."

And are we ever good at keeping it alive!

Runaway Fear

We may have valid fears, such as how we'll be able to pay our bills or how to keep our children from running into traffic. But even those fears can get away from us. Fear in general, both rational and irrational, tends to gain a life of its own and run at full speed, dragging us along with it. When it has us in its grip, it makes us feel out of control, as if we are hanging on to a runaway horse. We clutch it with all our might and hope and pray we won't fall off.

Yes, there are things that rightfully cause anxiety in this life, but often those things get blown out of proportion if we camp on them. We take something that is a valid worry and blow it up to huge proportions. Then we build our home on it, making it the foundation of our waking and sleeping hours. Nothing we do is outside of that worry and it dominates our thoughts, even when we are carrying out our everyday duties.

We tend to not only grab onto fear but feed it, as if it's a hungry tiger that can never be satiated. In the idle places of our minds, we let it take hold and slowly take over more and more of our inner thoughts.

I love the humor with which Jodi Picoult approaches anxiety in her book *Sing You Home*: "Anxiety's like a rocking chair. It gives you something to do, but it doesn't get you very far."

And yet we rock like mad.

So What's the Answer?

The first step is to recognize our fears and anxieties. Only when we see them for what they are can we begin to put them in their proper place. Yann Martel wrote a book called *Life of Pi*, which is fictional tale about a man stuck in a small boat with a tiger. The main character of this tale says:

> "I must say a word about fear. It is life's only true opponent. Only fear can defeat life. It is a clever, treacherous adversary, how well I know. It has no decency, respects no law or convention, shows no mercy. It goes for your weakest spot, which it finds with unnerving ease. It begins in your mind, always . . . so you must fight hard to express it. You must fight hard to shine the light of words upon it. Because if you don't, if your fear becomes a wordless darkness that you avoid, perhaps even manage to forget, you open yourself to further attacks of fear because you never truly fought the opponent who defeated you."

So the first step is to recognize the fears that have become so wrapped around our personalities that we don't even acknowledge them anymore. Unless we face them squarely, we punch vaguely at the air, trying to fight what we sense is there—but since we have no idea what they are, we're just wasting energy.

But how do we do that? How do we pull up the roots of fear that have so firmly embedded themselves in our hearts and minds that we can't even imagine existing without them?

They have become so central to our daily existence that the mere thought of ridding ourselves of them causes us to fret. As a result, our lives become consumed with anxiety. It is the master and we are the helpless servants.

This book is about pulling up those roots. For many of us, they are so deep that we have no idea how to begin entangling them from our daily thoughts.

If you are like me and suffer from fear and anxiety, you have probably read a lot about it. You recognize the truth of what various writers say, and yet you struggle with how to implement their wisdom. If that is the case, taking 40 days to uproot this muddle is reasonable. After all, it's taken a lifetime to grow your anxiety, so it makes sense that it will take a concerted effort over time to untangle the mess you've made.

So you need to pull up roots, but you also need to become intimately aware of who God is and what he wants to do in your life. Only as you turn over your fears to a God who loves you and cares for you will you have freedom from the anxieties that plague you.

Over 40 days, you can take a closer look at the misconceptions you've had about God and face the fact that you've been trying to take his job, living under the illusion that you can actually master your fears and worries on your own.

Corrie ten Boom, a woman whose writings have had a profound effect in my life, said, "Worrying is carrying tomorrow's load with today's strength—carrying two days at once. It is moving into tomorrow ahead of time. Worrying doesn't empty tomorrow of its sorrow, it empties today of its strength." She was able to say this in spite of being interned in the Nazi concentration camp where her sister died.

As you embark on this journey of overcoming your fear and

anxiety, embrace the dichotomy of Frederick Buechner's wisdom in his book *Beyond Words*: "Here is the world. Beautiful and terrible things will happen. Don't be afraid."

Preparation for the
40-Day Journey

My granddaughter inherited my good imagination. When she was three years old, she was afraid of everything. She feared that wild animals lurked in the dining room when the lights were off, that the next page in the storybook was going to show a cat scratching a dog (we skipped that page), and that any food other than peanut butter would poison her.

Of course, we know those fears are ridiculous. Most of us go through life never worrying about carnivores in the house, are able to read about interactions between animal species without batting an eye, and eat a wide variety of foods. But looking at her fears has made me wonder what our fears look like to God. Are our fears just as silly to him? Does he take our immaturity into account just as I do with my granddaughter?

Such fears remind me of Leviticus 26:36: "You will live in such fear that the sound of a leaf driven by the wind will send you fleeing. You will run as though fleeing from a sword, and you will fall even when no one pursues you" (NLT).

That verse describes the fear I lived with for years. Nevertheless, fear is a universal human emotion. David says in Psalm 55:4–6, "My heart pounds in my chest. . . . Fear and trembling overwhelm me, and I can't stop shaking. Oh, that I had wings like a dove, then I would fly away and rest" (NLT).

Have you felt that way at times? Felt fear so palpable that it affected you physically, and you wanted simply to flee?

Yet there are valid things to fear: loss of a job, possessions, health, family, and even life. So how can we deal with our natural fear?

David goes on to say in Psalm 55:16–18, "But I will call on God, and the LORD will rescue me. Morning, noon, and night I cry out in my distress, and the LORD hears my voice. He ransoms me and keeps me safe from the battle waged against me" (NLT).

Note that battle waged against David. God didn't stop the battle— it still roared on around him. God doesn't always change our circumstances. We may pray that he heal our cancer, deliver us from bankruptcy, or protect us from harm during war, but he doesn't always do that.

So how can crying out to him all day help us with our fears? It reminds us that we can trust God and his never-failing love and character, even if he doesn't change our circumstances. David goes on to say in Psalm 55:22, "Give your burdens to the LORD, and he will take care of you. He will not permit the godly to slip and fall" (NLT). Though David's words seem contradictory, the truth is that even when we do slip and fall, God is still faithful to us. We can trust his care, even when that care doesn't deliver us from our difficulties.

We have a choice about how to handle our fear. We can let it paralyze us, or we can surrender what we cannot control to God and decide to move forward in faith—camping on the certainty that no matter what happens, God loves us. In Romans 8:38, the apostle Paul writes, "I am convinced that nothing can ever separate us from God's love. Neither death nor life, neither angels nor demons, neither our fears for today nor our worries about tomorrow—not even the powers of hell can separate us from God's love" (NLT).

Nothing could be better than a good, wise Father who loves us so much that he's working way beyond our understanding to bring us the best—he's behind the scenes working on our behalf, even in the midst of our fears. If that's the case, then we really do have nothing to fear.

The Way Out of Our Fear Is to Fear God

G. K. Chesterton said, "We fear men so much, because we fear God so little. One fear cures another." As counterintuitive as it seems, getting rid of our fear starts with fearing God.

I often hear people explain the fear of the Lord as a mere respect or reverence. But the Bible uses the word *fear* at least 300 times in reference to God, so it's a mistake to downplay it. The subject becomes even more mysterious when we read something like 1 John 4:18, which says "perfect love expels all fear." So how do we understand this dichotomy? How can we fear God while he expels all fear?

Scripture is full of examples of how fearing God is a positive, rather than negative, thing. For example, in Genesis 42:18, Joseph wins his brothers' trust when he declares he is a God-fearing man. It was because the midwives feared God that they obeyed him instead of the authorities and spared the Hebrew babies (Ex. 1:17). Pharaoh brought disaster on his nation because he did not fear God (Ex. 9:29–31). Moses chose leaders to help him on the condition that they feared God and wouldn't take bribes (Ex. 18:21), and he told the Hebrews that God met with them in a terrifying display of his power so they wouldn't sin (Ex. 20:20). The Mosaic Law cites fear of God as a reason to treat the disabled and elderly well (Lev. 19:14, 32). And lest you think this is only an Old Testament idea, note that Jesus states this more strongly than anyone when he says, "Don't be afraid of those who want to kill your body; they cannot touch your soul. Fear only God, who can destroy both soul and body in hell" (Matt. 10:28, NIV). Paul says to work toward complete holiness because we fear God (2 Cor. 7:1).

It's clear from these passages that fearing God is good because it saves us from caving in to our own sinful nature. That's why hearing that someone is God-fearing actually makes us trust that person more. If they fear God, they are more likely to keep their word and treat others with kindness. In fact, Romans 3, a classic chapter on sin, says our chief sin is that we "have no fear of God at all" (v. 18).

So how does fear of God, who is perfect love, take away fear? Most of us presume that evil in the world is the ultimate threat. If we are Christians, we may think that God is there to offset that evil somehow. But this is backward!

God is far scarier than any evil the world can throw at us. The evil in the world pales to nothing compared to the power of God. But although God is scary, he is only scary to evil. William D. Eisenhower put it this way in his article "Fearing God" in *Christianity Today*: "As I walk with the Lord, I discover that God poses an ominous threat to my ego, but not to me. He rescues me from my delusions, so he may reveal the truth that sets me free. . . . Fear of the Lord is the beginning of wisdom, but love from the Lord is its completion."

That love is demonstrated most clearly in Jesus Christ, who vanquished the power of evil through his death on the cross. By laying down his life for us, he showed that no matter how evil man can be, God's love for us is far, far greater.

How to Proceed

Therefore, the way out of fear is to root ourselves firmly in who God is. By understanding his character, we learn to trust him with the daily details of our lives.

That's why this book takes 40 days to examine God's attributes. As we gain insight into who he is, we are flooded with the truth that he cares for us and intends good for us, and this takes the place of the lies that our imaginations conjure up.

I highly recommend that once you start this book, you take it seriously enough to complete it. Set aside the entire 40 days and don't give up until you've seen it through. If you abandon it part way in, you may not achieve victory over your fear.

Also, although you can make great strides in overcoming fear, you may still have to deal with anxiety if that's part of your personality. I am an anxious person and am convinced that is something I will have to submit to Christ over and over again. I no longer am bound by constant imaginary fears, but I still feel anxiety regularly. I feel anxious when I have to meet new people, be in charge of an event, meet a deadline, or counsel someone in distress.

However, I am slowly learning to give those things to God rather than carrying them with me. It is a lifelong process, but the practice of realizing that only God is totally competent is slowly freeing me more and more. I hope that will be the case for you too.

Here are some other things that may help you as you set aside these 40 days:

As much as possible, surround yourself with healthy people.

It may be helpful to let go of some of the stressors in your life during the 40 days of dealing with your fears. For example, I mentored difficult people who were really hurting, and met with others mostly for work purposes. But during the 40 days, I began to go out with friends for fun and not just to work on some project together. As I reconnected with people I enjoyed, my spirit soared. It was great to spend time with friends for no other purpose than to have fun. These friends showed me that being committed to Christ doesn't take away our joy but multiplies it exponentially—something I really needed as I faced my fears.

This also meant that I needed to quit meeting with really broken people for a time. I recognized that I might be able to do that again someday, but at that point I needed to be with emotionally healthy people.

Of course, there are some unhealthy people we just can't avoid. If you live or work with such people, this 40-day exercise will help you cope with them more wisely and graciously.

It's okay to say no.

During the 40 days, I decided not to take on anything extra so I would have the time and energy to deal with my fears. I trusted that if God wanted me to say yes to any commitments, he would make it abundantly clear. That decision helped me see how guilt, instead of God, often drove me to say yes to things people asked of me. It also showed me that fear of what others thought of me was a driving factor in my life.

This meant that when someone at church asked me to be on the care team, I politely declined and suggested a friend who has the gift of mercy. When our church children's director asked me to teach a class, I said no but suggested a friend who loves to work with children.

When someone from my community's international ministry asked if I could house students, I said no but suggested friends who love that ministry. In the past I said yes to all those things not because I felt called to them but because I could see the need—and felt it was up to me to meet it (part of my tendency toward being overly responsible—and my irrational fear of saying no).

When the 40 days were up, I felt the freedom to start saying yes to things and to do things that I didn't have the courage for before. For example, we temporarily housed a young man who was trying to start a campus ministry. I said yes to that because I felt no burden, only joy, when I prayed about it.

Of course, I still have to obey God and do some things that are difficult for me. When I was asked to speak at our women's retreat, my gut reaction was to say no. But when I prayed about it, God gave me all sorts of ideas I felt he wanted me to share. Though speaking is never fun for me, I felt encouraged that what I shared was useful to others.

I knew I was making progress when a friend told me excitedly about her call to mission work in Africa. I rejoiced that God had called her to such a great and important ministry, but did not confuse her call for mine—something I would have done when fear still consumed my life.

Deal with demanding Scriptures and let them change you.

This 40-day approach is deeply rooted in the Bible, and it may cause you to think about familiar passages differently.

When I first recognized that I had a problem with fear, I had trouble reading the New Testament because all I saw there were challenges to mission, which fed into my fear that I wasn't doing enough. I just wanted to read Psalms because they comforted me. This was okay at first, but I knew I had to get back to the New Testament eventually. I recognized that God's Word is true—it was my reading of it that was off, so I had to figure out how to deal with the demanding things there.

For example, some of the passages I struggled with were ones such as Philippians 2:17: "Even if I am being poured out as a drink offering on the sacrifice and service coming from your faith, I am glad and rejoice with all of you" (NIV). As I look at this verse now, I realize Paul was saying that he was being poured out as a drink offering—and God was doing the pouring. Somehow I had twisted this into the idea that I had to endlessly pour my life out as a drink offering—and I did so to the point of exhaustion.

Or Matthew 25:31–46, where Jesus tells us that if we do something for the hungry, thirsty, stranger, sick, or those in prison, we do it for him. I interpreted this to mean that I had to ferret out every person who had such needs so I could personally meet them. There is nothing in this passage that tells me otherwise, but I tried it and couldn't do it. So as I read this now, I take it to mean that if such a person crosses my path, God has sent them to me and I have a responsibility to help them or find someone else to do so (something I never did before). However, if I go looking for such people in our modern world, I'm quickly overwhelmed by needs I can't possibly keep up with, especially since I receive daily reminders of those needs in my mailbox and inbox.

When I started walking with Christ in my early 20s, I listened to an elderly man explain why he was going on a dangerous mission trip. "I'd rather wear out than rust out," he said.

I loved that! And I still do. However, what that translated to in my funny little brain was that I had to expend myself beyond my endurance (how else was I going to wear out?).

Perhaps my biggest fear has been that when I get to heaven, instead of saying, "Well done, my good and faithful servant" (Matt. 25:23), God will say, "What were you doing down there?" I want to know that my life counts for something here on earth. So doesn't it make sense to give, and give, and give, until my last ounce of strength is gone? Isn't that being a good steward of what God gave me? After all, that's how I'd approach being a good steward of my finances, creation, or my workplace, so why not use the same approach when I think about my body?

But is that the approach I'd take for finances, creation, or my workplace? No! I'd consider it irresponsible to spend every dime rather than saving some for a rainy day or retirement. I'd never think that using up creation was okay. I want to conserve it to my best ability. And if my workplace demanded every ounce of my strength at the expense of my family and ministry, I'd have a long talk with my boss.

Many years and much maturing later, I have some perspective on Philippians 2:7. I realize that Paul was saying that if God poured him out as a drink offering, he'd count it joy. He didn't pour himself out as a drink offering. That's just crazy, unnecessary, and even disobedient.

And about the "well done" part? Who wants a servant who does other than what he's told? What if you hired someone to clean your house and instead he washed all your neighbors' cars? He might even brag that he got five more washed this week than last. So what? You hired him to clean your house. A good servant does what he's asked to do, not whatever he can find to do. I'm sure the number of dirty cars is infinite, but that's not his job.

An important part of my healing has been reading these demanding passages with "new eyes" so I can once more love the whole Word of God and find freedom from my irrational fears.

Accept God's good gifts.

Along with letting go of my fears, I learned to embrace God's many blessings. Over the 40 days, I asked him to open my eyes to his goodness so I could soak it all in. God's grace is amazing, and I don't deserve anything he gives me. Every blessing and victory I experience are by his goodness.

Not only were my fears vanquished through those 40 days, but my prayer life was revolutionized. Instead of agonizing over my friend's wayward son, I rejoiced that God loves him, is holding on to him, and will never let him go. Instead of being miserable about a family member's broken marriage, I rejoiced that God still loves her and is constantly wooing her. This attitude of praise turned everything around, because I saw God working everywhere—even when there was no visible evidence of it.

The 40 days ushered me into a new phase of enjoying God. Instead of constantly wondering what I should be doing for him, I just enjoyed being in his presence. I loved listening for his voice and delighting in what he has made me for and called me to do.

How This Book Is Organized

Each morning of the 40-day journey starts with a Scripture passage, a short meditation on that passage, and a prayer.

Then each evening, you will revisit your day and think about how things went. If you didn't do as well as you'd hoped, don't be discouraged. That's why there are 40 days to this journey! You have plenty more days to practice giving your anxiety to God.

Finally, I would like to add that if you have a clinically diagnosed anxiety disorder, this method may or may not work for you. There could be other, more complex things at play. Regardless, it will be useful to immerse yourself in learning who God is and to work through some of the things that cause you anxiety. If, however, you find that you're unable to shake your fears, you may need to seek professional help.

Day 1: Who Is God?

Loving

A.M. Meditation

Scripture Passage

God showed how much he loved us by sending his one and only Son into the world so that we might have eternal life through him. This is real love—not that we loved God, but that he loved us and sent his Son as a sacrifice to take away our sins. Dear friends, since God loved us that much, we surely ought to love each other. No one has ever seen God. But if we love each other, God lives in us, and his love is brought to full expression in us. And God has given us his Spirit as proof that we live in him and he in us. Furthermore, we have seen with our own eyes and now testify that the Father sent his Son to be the Savior of the world. All who declare that Jesus is the Son of God have God living in them, and they live in God. We know how much God loves us, and we have put our trust in his love. God is love, and all who live in love live in God, and God lives in them. And as we live in God, our love grows more perfect. So we will not be afraid on the day of judgment, but we can face him with confidence because we live like Jesus here in this world. Such love has no fear, because perfect love expels all fear. If we are afraid, it is for fear of punishment, and this shows that we have not fully experienced his perfect love. (1 John 4:9–18, NLT)

Meditation

The apostle John gives us great insight into who God is. In the Gospel he wrote, John calls himself "the disciple whom Jesus loved" throughout the narrative, defining his very identity by his relationship with Christ. And in this passage, he doesn't merely say that God is full of love, but that God *is* love. In other words, the word *love* is defined by God and is meaningless without him.

How does he know that God is love? He says at the very beginning of this passage, "This is real love—not that we loved God, but that he loved us and sent his Son as a sacrifice to take away our sins." As one of his disciples while he was on earth, John already had a good sense of Jesus' love for him, but it must have blown him away when he realized that Jesus went to the Cross for him—that his sins were entirely washed away in that moment of supreme sacrifice.

So how does knowing that God loves us help us let go of our fears? It helps us to know we have a safe place to land—that no matter what happens to us, God is surrounding us with his perfect love.

In this passage, John says, "We know how much God loves us, and we have put our trust in his love." As we soak up the magnitude of how much God loves us, it becomes easier to trust that he is caring for us no matter how difficult our circumstances.

Not only can we be free of fear in the midst of difficulty, but we are also free from any kind of fear of God. As John makes clear, "Such love has no fear, because perfect love expels all fear. If we are afraid, it is for fear of punishment, and this shows that we have not fully experienced his perfect love."

That is your goal today—to soak up God's perfect love and to really believe it. Each time you feel anxious or begin to worry about something, let God's love wash over you. Memorize the phrase "Such love has no fear," and keep it at the forefront of your thoughts as you go about your day. It may even be helpful to take a deep breath and say that phrase aloud to yourself when you confront something that makes you particularly anxious.

Prayer

Lord, help me to truly understand that you never act outside of your love. You always surround me with your care and you will never abandon me for a moment. Help me to recognize my fears today and keep me centered on your love so that I can experience freedom from worry.

P.M. Meditation

How did things go today? Were you able to remember God's love in the midst of your fears and worries? Were you able to hand them to him and know that because of his love you can trust him with all the details of your life? If not, do so now. Take a deep breath and picture yourself handing all your cares to him. Now rest well.

Day 2: Who Is God?

Faithful

A.M. Meditation

Scripture Passage

Your unfailing love, O LORD, is as vast as the heavens;

  your faithfulness reaches beyond the clouds.

Your righteousness is like the mighty mountains,

  your justice like the ocean depths.

You care for people and animals alike, O LORD.

  How precious is your unfailing love, O God!

All humanity finds shelter

  in the shadow of your wings.

You feed them from the abundance of your own house,

letting them drink from your river of delights.

For you are the fountain of life,

the light by which we see. (Ps. 36:5–9, NLT)

Meditation

Yesterday we looked at God's love, and today we see that his faithfulness is directly tied to his perfect love. Because of his love, he is faithful to us, even if we don't deserve it. His love is as "vast as the heavens," so his faithfulness "reaches beyond the clouds."

He cares for people and animals alike. I love that animals are included in his care because that confirms that his love is constant, even when we do nothing to earn it. Animals know nothing of God's commands and cannot worship him as we do, and yet his care extends to them.

All humanity finds shelter in the shadow of his wings. This brings to mind Jesus' words about Jerusalem in Matthew 23:37, where he says, "How often I have wanted to gather your children together as a hen protects her chicks beneath her wings, but you wouldn't let me." That seems to indicate that the only condition to being under his shelter is a willingness to be so. As we put ourselves in his care, he will protect us beyond our own ability to do so.

The last few verses of this passage concern God's faithfulness to provide for us. With phrases such as "feed them from the abundance of your house," we are assured that he knows our needs and will supply them. I think of the time my husband was in seminary, and because of medical bills we had no money for groceries the last week of the month. Together we had less than twenty-five cents. As we wondered what we could possibly do, we received a letter from a woman I had met randomly over seven years before. She sent a small check, saying, "I heard your husband was in seminary and thought you could use this." It was just enough to buy things like oatmeal, bread, peanut butter, and apples. Our kids were thrilled that I didn't make them eat a single vegetable all week, and it has remained a benchmark in trusting God for our needs.

Finally, the psalmist says, "For you are the fountain of life, the light by which we see." God is faithful because his very nature is to be so. He is bubbling over with life and is light itself (see Rev. 22:5). That can only result in faithfulness that spills over and lights up our lives. Keep the phrase "you are the fountain of life" at the forefront of your thoughts today.

Prayer

I am willing to put myself in your care, Lord. I believe you are faithful and that you long to gather me under your wings to protect and care for me. I place myself there and ask you to help me be mindful of that care throughout the day, no matter what I face. Remind me when I run away from your care and shoulder things on my own, trying to control my circumstances as fear overwhelms me. When those moments happen, quietly draw me back into your shelter and reassure me of your faithfulness to me.

P.M. Meditation

Did you stay in his shelter and care today when fear and anxiety threatened? Did you remain aware of his faithfulness? If not, rest in his shelter right now. Picture yourself firmly in his arms, protected from all harm. Rest well as you place yourself willingly in his care.

Day 3: Who Is God?

Joyful

A.M. Meditation

Scripture Passage

Declare me innocent, O God!

Defend me against these ungodly people.

Rescue me from these unjust liars.

For you are God, my only safe haven.

Why have you tossed me aside?

Why must I wander around in grief,

oppressed by my enemies?

Send out your light and your truth;

let them guide me.

Let them lead me to your holy mountain,

to the place where you live.

There I will go to the altar of God,

to God—the source of all my joy.

I will praise you with my harp,

O God, my God!

Why am I discouraged?

Why is my heart so sad?

I will put my hope in God!

I will praise him again—

my Savior and my God! (Ps. 43, NLT)

Meditation

At first glance, this psalm may not seem to be about joy. However, as we look closer, the very contrasts make it so. The psalmist is in despair. His reputation is apparently under attack from ungodly people who are spreading lies about him. In the midst of that, he declares God as his only safe haven. We can imagine the helplessness and fear that come from being falsely accused. I have had that happen a few times in my life, but only on a small scale (mostly I have deserved any accusations that have come my way!). But I remember the initial feeling of indignation, which gave way to fear that others would believe the false accusation against me. Circumstances felt completely out of my control and anxiety reigned as I realized I could do nothing to change the situation.

It's so bad for the psalmist that he feels God has tossed him aside. He wanders around in grief and is oppressed by his enemies. But now that he has his despair on the table, he can deal with it. His very honesty is the doorway to finding hope and deliverance from his desperate feelings. As he admits them, he asks God to send out his light and truth to guide him—to lead him to his holy mountain, the place where he lives. In other words, he wants to be in God's presence.

Why does he want to be in God's presence? Because God is the source of all his joy. As we talked about God being love, so is he joy.

Even though the psalmist is struggling with his emotions of fear and discouragement, he chooses to praise God with his harp. As he expresses the feelings that threaten to overwhelm and swamp him, he forces himself to look beyond his natural reactions and to seek Truth. Asking himself why he is sad and discouraged, he determines to put his hope in God. "I will praise him again—my savior and my God!"

As fear and anxiety threaten you today, commit the phrase "God—the source of all my joy" to memory. When circumstances or fear and anxiety start to overwhelm you, place yourself firmly in God's presence, your source of all joy.

Prayer

Lord, it is so easy for me to pretend I have things under control. I can tell myself things are no big deal, but then that lie will crush me under its weight. Help me to recognize when I am stuffing my anxiety. Help me to see why I am feeling anxious and to deal with it head on instead of pretending I don't feel overwhelmed. After I identify my fear, help me to run to your presence, the source of all my joy.

P.M. Meditation

Were you able to identify your anxieties today? Did you notice more than you did on the previous days? If so, were you able to place yourself in God's hands and leave your anxiety with him? If not, name each anxiety he revealed to you today and leave them with him now. Trust that he is the very definition of joy, and rest in his presence tonight.

Day 4: Who Is God?

Kind

A.M. Meditation

Scripture Passage

Please, Lord, remember,

    you have always

    been patient and kind.

Forget each wrong I did

    when I was young.

      Show how truly kind you are

    and remember me.

You are honest and merciful,

    and you teach sinners

how to follow your path.

You lead humble people

to do what is right

and to stay on your path.

In everything you do,

you are kind and faithful

to everyone who keeps

our agreement with you.

Be true to your name, Lord,

by forgiving each one

of my terrible sins.

You will show the right path

to all who worship you.

They will have plenty,

and then their children

will receive the land. (Ps. 25:6–13, CEV)

Meditation

According to the *Cambridge Dictionary*, to be kind means to be "generous, helpful, and caring about other people." We've all experienced kindness from others, and we recognize it most clearly when we've suffered, been persecuted, or are generally feeling low. So it makes sense that we'd most easily recognize God's kindness at those times. As the psalmist mentions, he realizes how kind the Lord is to him when he thinks about his sin.

I fail to see God's kindness to me when I dwell on the fact that I didn't get something I wanted. But if I instead dwell on all the ways he has cared for me even when I have been unfaithful and disobedient, I am bowled over by his kindness to me.

Keeping God's kindness in mind is tremendously helpful as I deal with my fear. A lot of my fear stems from the fact that I believe God *can* keep me and those I love safe, but I'm not sure he *will* do so. When I am plagued with those kinds of doubts and fears, I need to remember God's intention toward me is to always be kind. No matter what I am going through, his kindness is central to my future. He will *always* act out of that kindness and will never fail to do so in any way.

When I keep that in mind, this particular attribute of God is able to penetrate my overwhelming and all-consuming fears. He wants to be kind to me. He wants to show me how kind he is. He will never be anything but kind to me. Keeping those truths in mind allows me to trust him and to look hopefully upon my day.

Let these words from the psalm—"you have always been patient and kind"—be your mantra today. Ask God to make you aware of when you are feeling anxious and fearful. In that moment, recite that phrase and let it soak deep into your bones.

Prayer

Lord, help me to understand that you long to show me kindness, but that I am often too bound up in my fears and anxiety to recognize it. Open my eyes to your kindness today. Help me to notice it in the big things and the small things. Even when things don't go my way, help me to experience your kindness in the midst of the chaos. Help me to recognize that you have always been patient and kind and that nothing will ever change that.

P.M. Meditation

Is it becoming easier or more difficult to recognize when you are being anxious and fearful? Is it opening the proverbial can of worms? As you are recognizing your fear more, are you realizing that other areas of your life are filled with anxiety? If so, that is good! One of the principal keys to dealing with our anxiety is recognizing and naming it. We can't overcome something we don't fully understand. So thank God that he is revealing these areas to you, and rejoice that he will help you conquer them one by one. Now rest well tonight, knowing that God is always patient and kind.

Day 5: Who Is God?

Gentle

A.M. Meditation

Scripture Passage

Then Jesus began to denounce the towns where he had done so many of his miracles, because they hadn't repented of their sins and turned to God. "What sorrow awaits you, Korazin and Bethsaida! For if the miracles I did in you had been done in wicked Tyre and Sidon, their people would have repented of their sins long ago, clothing themselves in burlap and throwing ashes on their heads to show their remorse. I tell you, Tyre and Sidon will be better off on judgment day than you.

"And you people of Capernaum, will you be honored in heaven? No, you will go down to the place of the dead. For if the miracles I did for you had been done in wicked Sodom, it would still be here today. I tell you, even Sodom will be better off on judgment day than you."

At that time Jesus prayed this prayer: "O Father, Lord of heaven and earth, thank you for hiding these things from those who think themselves wise and clever, and for revealing them to the childlike. Yes, Father, it pleased you to do it this way!

"My Father has entrusted everything to me. No one truly knows the Son except the Father, and no one truly knows the Father except the Son and those to whom the Son chooses to reveal him."

Then Jesus said, "Come to me, all of you who are weary and carry heavy burdens, and I will give you rest. Take my yoke upon you. Let me teach you, because I am humble and gentle at heart, and you will find rest for your souls. For my yoke is easy to bear, and the burden I give you is light." (Matt. 11:20–30, NLT)

Meditation

When you began reading today's Scripture passage, you must have thought, *What in the world does this have to do with gentleness?* I mean, Jesus is calling out these people from Korazin, Bethsaida, and Capernaum because they did not repent of their sins when he did amazing things among them. He gave them chances others didn't have, and yet they rejected him.

It sounds like an angry and bitter tirade, but we find Jesus has far different motives as he talks about his connection to the Father, explaining how he represents the Father while on earth. His motive is to wake up those who are blind to him and to invite them in; immediately after this pronouncement of judgment, he throws his arms open wide and invites everyone who is weary and carries heavy burdens to come to him. He promises rest, something most of us long for.

Then he says something that is strange to our modern ears: "Take my yoke upon you." A yoke was a device for draft animals (especially oxen and horses) that joined them together. That idea is where we get the modern idea of horsepower. Two horses together have a lot more power than one by itself. In this passage, Jesus is offering to be yoked with us. He will take the lion's share of the pulling and provide rest when we need it. He pleads with us to let him do this as he teaches us. And why should we trust his teaching? Because he is humble and gentle of heart.

So what does this have to do with our fears? Fear and anxiety are extremely heavy burdens. They weigh us down constantly; they dominate our waking hours and disturb our sleeping hours. We feel that we are yoked to a runaway horse that is dragging us through the mud. Jesus asks us to trade that runaway horse for him. He tells us that his yoke is easy to bear and that the burden he gives us is light. Why? Because he is taking on the heavy part of the burden, giving us a chance to rest.

As you go about your day, keep the phrase "my yoke is easy to bear" at the forefront of your mind. When you face something that causes fear or anxiety, repeat that phrase and picture Jesus—who describes himself as humble and gentle—taking care of the problem. He's got this!

Prayer

Jesus, I know you are humble and gentle. That is part of what draws me to you. You long to take my burden and lighten my load. I ask you to remind me of this throughout the day. As I feel the weight of my fears, I pray that you'll remind me that your yoke is easy to bear, and that you'll gently lift the load from my shoulders and take it upon your own.

P.M. Meditation

Were you aware of what you were "yoked" to today? Did you stay yoked to your fears or did you consciously allow Jesus into the yoke instead? If it didn't go so well, now is a wonderful time to firmly place yourself in his care. If you do so, he promises you rest, something that we all need at the end of the day. Go to sleep confident that Jesus is handling your burdens so that you can rest in him.

Day 6: Who Is God?

Ever-present

A.M. Meditation

Scripture Passage

O Lord, you have examined my heart

  and know everything about me.

You know when I sit down or stand up.

  You know my thoughts even when I'm far away.

You see me when I travel

  and when I rest at home.

  You know everything I do.

You know what I am going to say

  even before I say it, Lord.

You go before me and follow me.

   You place your hand of blessing on my head.

Such knowledge is too wonderful for me,

   too great for me to understand!

I can never escape from your Spirit!

   I can never get away from your presence!

If I go up to heaven, you are there;

   if I go down to the grave, you are there.

If I ride the wings of the morning,

   if I dwell by the farthest oceans,

even there your hand will guide me,

   and your strength will support me.

I could ask the darkness to hide me

   and the light around me to become night—

   but even in darkness I cannot hide from you.

To you the night shines as bright as day.

   Darkness and light are the same to you. (Ps. 139:1–12, NLT)

Meditation

Far too often, the fact that God is ever-present has been used in a negative way in Christendom. I know many who are terrified by this prospect because they see him as a fierce judge who is staring at them, waiting for them to mess up. But that is not the intent of this psalm. It is meant to be an encouragement.

If you are terrified of God's presence, these 40 days will help you gain a right view of God so that you'll feel safe, rather than threatened, in his presence.

The beginning of this psalm can rattle us because we realize that we can't put anything over on God. Although we may fool others, he knows everything we are thinking. In spite of that, God loves us and wants to enter into our thoughts—even when they are wretched. As the psalmist says, "You go before me and follow me. You place your hand of blessing on my head. Such knowledge is too wonderful for me, too great for me to understand!"

Note that even though God knows all your thoughts, he places his hand of blessing on your head. The psalmist is so bowled over by this that he can't quite get a grasp on it. It's amazing to him. In today's vernacular, we might say, "You follow me, you surround me, and you keep your hand on me. I can hardly believe this! It's more than I can take in! You never, ever let go of me, even when I mess up."

The image is of a loving parent with a very young child, keeping a firm hand on her to keep her safe, stroking her head to help her get to sleep at night, doing everything possible to make sure she is loved and cared for. Even when she is defiant, even when she is completely unlikeable, the parent loves her.

So whether we travel, rest at home, ride the wings of the morning, dwell by the farthest oceans—even if we go down to the grave—God is there. And he's a loving God who cares about us and wants to carry us through our toughest times.

What does this mean for our fears? We are never alone! He will never leave us for a moment.

I have found this especially comforting when I am alone and afraid.

My imagination can conjure up all sorts of disasters, but what I'm learning to do is to instead imagine that Jesus is right beside me, because he is!

In a strange little book called *God Guides*, Mary Geegh—a missionary to India in the early 1900s—tells the story of when she received a death threat. That night she locked her door and sat home alone, terrified to her core. Finally, as she prayed about it, she gained confidence that God was with her. With that in mind, she unlocked the door and went to sleep. Nothing happened, and her fear was conquered in a way it wouldn't have been otherwise. Now, I'm not advising that we leave our doors unlocked, but this woman needed to do so. By trusting God to keep her safe, she was able to banish her fear and find peace.

Keep the phrase "To you the night shines as bright as day" at the forefront of your mind today, and enjoy God's presence.

Prayer

Lord, make me aware of your presence throughout this day. Help me to picture you at my side, protecting me every moment. I ask that when I am fearful you'll remind me that you have promised, "I will never fail you. I will never abandon you" (Heb. 13:5, NLT). When my pulse races and I feel anxiety rising, help me to be aware that you are with me and want to care for me.

P.M. Meditation

As you wind down your day, rest in God's presence. Let your fears go as if they are being blown away by the wind. Take a deep breath, and picture the Holy Spirit within you giving you courage and strength. Imagine that Jesus is next to you, caring for you as a loving parent cares for a child, and rest well in that knowledge.

Day 7: Who Is God?

Peaceful

A.M. Meditation

Scripture Passage

Rejoice in the Lord always. I will say it again: Rejoice! Let your gentleness be evident to all. The Lord is near. Do not be anxious about anything, but in every situation, by prayer and petition, with thanksgiving, present your requests to God. And the peace of God, which transcends all understanding, will guard your hearts and your minds in Christ Jesus.

Finally, brothers and sisters, whatever is true, whatever is noble, whatever is right, whatever is pure, whatever is lovely, whatever is admirable—if anything is excellent or praiseworthy—think about such things. Whatever you have learned or received or heard from me, or seen in me—put it into practice. And the God of peace will be with you. (Phil. 4:4–7, NIV)

Meditation

This passage in Philippians gives us a strong description of God's peace. It starts with telling us to rejoice. When we are lacking peace, that is probably the last thing we feel like doing, yet that is what we are instructed to do. Why should we rejoice? Because "the Lord is near." All anxiety flees when you recognize that the God of peace is with you and never leaves your side, just as we reflected on in yesterday's meditation.

Not only is he near, but when you trust him with whatever is causing you to be anxious, he promises to "guard your hearts and your minds in Christ Jesus." Only a God who embodies peace can do that, and in the process he'll fill you with a peace that transcends understanding—in other words, beyond what makes sense in your circumstances.

The next paragraph follows that thought with encouragement to think about what is true, noble, right, pure, lovely, admirable, excellent, or praiseworthy. This is far more than positive thinking or dwelling on only the "sunny side of life." This is rooting yourself in who God is and what he is trying to accomplish in your life and on the earth. It's replacing all the garbage in this world with a God of peace who wants to assure you that he knows what he is doing and will bring about good in your life in spite of the difficulties you face. That should give you peace, because God is peace.

Even when we read about God judging wickedness in the Bible, we recognize that he is a God of peace. Romans 16:20 (NIV) says, "The God of peace will soon crush Satan under your feet." At first glance that seems like a contradiction. How can he be a God of peace while he is crushing Satan? But it actually makes perfect sense. If he is indeed a God of peace, of course he would crush the one whose goal is to shatter peace on earth (and in you).

As anxious thoughts hit you today, give them over to God

immediately. Personalize verse 7 as "the God of peace is with me," and say it to yourself when anxiety threatens you.

Prayer

Father, help me to know and deeply understand that you are peace. That means if I am feeling anxious about my circumstances, that anxiety is not from you. It is either from my own circular thinking or from the pit of hell. Help me to root myself firmly in you and therefore in your peace. No matter what happens today, help me to know that you are with me and intend good for me. Fill me with your peace, which I can only comprehend with your help.

P.M. Meditation

Were you able to recognize the times that anxiety threatened to overtake you? And if so, were you able to rest in our God of peace? If so, rejoice! If not, take time to do so now. Let all your anxieties drift to heaven and let God brush them away as if they're specks of dust. Now let his peace wash over you as you dwell on that which is excellent and praiseworthy.

Day 8: Who Is God?

Patient

A.M. Meditation

Scripture Passage

I thank Christ Jesus our Lord, who has given me strength to do his work. He considered me trustworthy and appointed me to serve him, even though I used to blaspheme the name of Christ. In my insolence, I persecuted his people. But God had mercy on me because I did it in ignorance and unbelief. Oh, how generous and gracious our Lord was! He filled me with the faith and love that come from Christ Jesus.

This is a trustworthy saying, and everyone should accept it: "Christ Jesus came into the world to save sinners"—and I am the worst of them all. But God had mercy on me so that Christ Jesus could use me as a prime example of his great patience with even the worst sinners. Then others will realize that they, too, can believe in him and receive eternal life. All honor and glory to God forever and ever! He is the eternal King, the unseen one who never dies; he alone is God. Amen. (1 Tim. 1:12–17, NLT)

Meditation

Paul is writing to Timothy in this passage, marveling that in spite of his dubious past as one who vilified Christ and persecuted Christians, God had mercy on him and had now appointed him to do his work. The wonder of that never leaves Paul. He recounts it in several of his letters—evidently astounded that God would not only forgive him but appoint him to serve. He says, "I am the worst of them all. But God had mercy on me so that Christ Jesus could use me as a prime example of his great patience with even the worst sinners."

I don't know what you've done, but it's unlikely that whatever it was is worse than what Paul did. He discounted Christ at every turn and was determined to wipe out all of Jesus' followers. And yet God was patient with him. He allowed him to blunder on in his misguided way until the exact right moment when Jesus confronted him and commissioned him with a new task. This affected Paul so thoroughly that he begins most of his letters by talking about the God of mercy and grace, even as he goes on to correct the churches in what they are doing wrong.

What does that have to do with our fears? If your fears have anything to do with how you've failed and fear failing again, this passage should give you great courage. God is patient. This is obvious not only from the New Testament but from the Old Testament as well. God was patient with Israel for centuries, even though they turned their back on him. His patience is not endless, and we should never think we can thumb our nose at him, but if we sincerely want to follow him he is remarkably patient with our failures.

As you go through your day, ask God to reveal the ways that you fear failure. And when he does, ask him if that is limiting how you can live for him and how you experience victory over your fears. Memorize the phrase "God had mercy on me," and say it to yourself when you feel you've messed up once again.

Prayer

God of mercy and patience, help me to see you as you are rather than my faulty assumptions of who you are. Help me to see your great patience with me and that you understand I am a frail human being who can only become fearless as I let you be my strength. Let knowledge of your patience wash over me today so that I can be braver than I ever thought possible.

P.M. Meditation

Were you aware of God's mercy and patience today? Did you recognize the ways you are overly hard on yourself? Were you able to have victory today in at least one small thing that filled you with fear? Ask God to bring to mind any way you failed in that today, and let it soak in deeply that God is extremely patient with your frailties and can't wait to give you another chance tomorrow.

Day 9: Who Is God?

Good

A.M. Meditation

Scripture Passage

You, Lord, are forgiving and good,

    abounding in love to all who call to you.

Hear my prayer, Lord;

    listen to my cry for mercy.

When I am in distress, I call to you,

    because you answer me.

Among the gods there is none like you, Lord;

    no deeds can compare with yours.

All the nations you have made

will come and worship before you, Lord;

they will bring glory to your name.

For you are great and do marvelous deeds;

you alone are God.

Teach me your way, Lord,

that I may rely on your faithfulness;

give me an undivided heart,

that I may fear your name.

I will praise you, Lord my God, with all my heart;

I will glorify your name forever.

For great is your love toward me;

you have delivered me from the depths,

from the realm of the dead. (Ps. 86:5–13, NIV)

Meditation

The Psalms give us great insight into God's character. David wrote this one as a prayer, absorbing God's nature into his heart as he worked through the things that caused him agony. He acknowledges early in the psalm that God is good and forgiving.

That knowledge gave him confidence to trust him with the difficult things in his life. Because of that goodness, he could ask for mercy and know it would be granted. He could also trust him with his life when circumstances were wretched.

Many of my fears stem from my inability to truly believe God is good. I can't quite grasp that he always wants what is best for me. In the back of my mind, I think of him as a really powerful human, and humans always have a selfish bent—especially powerful humans. The fact that God wants glory is suspect in my mind. It smacks of an egomaniac who wants adulation to make up for the insecurities he feels.

But God is not human. He is so far above being a human that I can't really comprehend him. My earthly experience doesn't allow me to understand a being who is so beyond my imagination that when he asks me to give him glory, it's in my best interest as well. How do I know that? Because God is good and nothing he does is outside of that goodness.

When you face something you fear today, think of the phrase "You, Lord, are forgiving and good." And when you do call to him, know with confidence beyond your human experience that God is good and will act out of goodness no matter what fear you encounter.

Prayer

Heavenly Father, you are truly beyond my comprehension. Nothing I have ever experienced on this earth compares to you. Help me to get past all the ways I've thought of you wrongly in the past. Give me wisdom and strength to take the first step into the certainty that you are good and always act out of that goodness. No matter what I encounter today, remind me of that so I can trust you with what I fear.

P.M. Meditation

Did you think about God a bit differently today? Were you able to trust him more because you are confident that he is truly good? If not, trust him with that struggle and ask his help to reorient your thinking about him. As you dwell on his goodness, let your thoughts abide there as you renew your body and mind in rest.

Day 10: Who Is God?

Sovereign

A.M. Meditation

Scripture Passage

Pursue righteousness, godliness, faith, love, steadfastness, gentleness. Fight the good fight of the faith. Take hold of the eternal life to which you were called and about which you made the good confession in the presence of many witnesses. I charge you in the presence of God, who gives life to all things, and of Christ Jesus, who in his testimony before Pontius Pilate made the good confession, to keep the commandment unstained and free from reproach until the appearing of our Lord Jesus Christ, which he will display at the proper time—he who is the blessed and only Sovereign, the King of kings and Lord of lords, who alone has immortality, who dwells in unapproachable light, whom no one has ever seen or can see. To him be honor and eternal dominion. Amen. (1 Tim. 6:11b–16, ESV)

Meditation

The word *sovereign* is a strange word to our modern ears. Because most of us no longer live under a king, we are not used to someone having sovereignty over us. In fact, many of us rail against the idea. We like living in a democracy and have no desire to return to a feudal system.

Yet, as Paul says to Timothy in the passage we read today, God is sovereign over all things. He is the "King of kings and Lord of lords." He alone is immortal and "dwells in unapproachable light." And only to him belong "honor and eternal dominion." So what does that mean for my fears? It means I am not the master of my own fate as I long to be. It means that many things are out of my control; I need to face that squarely. But just because things are out of my control does not mean my life has to be chaotic.

In fact, it's just the opposite. Once I relinquish my tentative hold on things, I am able to trust the only one who truly controls everything. And that's a very great comfort.

The knowledge of God's sovereignty would not be comforting if we didn't believe the things we have already learned about his character. Because we know he is loving, faithful, joyful, kind, gentle, ever present, peaceful, patient, and good, we know we can trust him with all the details of our lives.

So what does that mean concerning our fears? It means we can trust him with whatever we fear. He is far greater than our fears and is truly in control when we are not. That knowledge allows us to unclench our fists, take a deep breath, and let the Holy Spirit comfort us with the certainty that the sovereign God will not fail us.

As you go through your day, keep in mind that God "dwells in unapproachable light." Let that light illuminate your fears and drive them away.

Prayer

"Sovereign . . . King of kings and Lord of lords, who alone has immortality, who dwells in unapproachable light, whom no one has ever seen or can see. To [you] be honor and eternal dominion. Amen."

P.M. Meditation

Were you able to keep in mind that God is sovereign over all things? Did you abide in the one who "dwells in unapproachable light"? If not, it's not too late. Identify your fears, and even as you turn off your light tonight to sleep, know that the one who defines light is watching over you.

Day 11: Who Is God?

Father

A.M. Meditation

Scripture Passage

Grace to you and peace from God our Father and the Lord Jesus Christ. Blessed be the God and Father of our Lord Jesus Christ, the Father of mercies and God of all comfort, who comforts us in all our affliction so that we will be able to comfort those who are in any affliction with the comfort with which we ourselves are comforted by God. (2 Cor. 1:2–4, NLT)

Meditation

Whether we should or not, we often think of God in terms of our earthly fathers. The trouble with this is that very few of us had fathers who were good at showing affection, and many more had fathers who were downright angry and abusive. Or perhaps your father was affectionate, but stepped over the bounds of that affection and took advantage of you. Or maybe he was a lot of fun, but failed to care and provide for you. The litany of bad fathers is almost endless. If that was your experience with a father, you will have to do the hard work of separating your involvement with your earthly father from the reality of life with your heavenly Father.

This is vitally important because you will not have confidence in God until you come to terms with the fact that he is a perfect Father. Our passage today says he is the "Father of mercies" and the "God of all comfort." That paints the picture of a God who is kind and gentle, not mean and vindictive. He is a God we can trust with the difficult things in our lives, because he is walking with us as we face them.

He's the kind of Father reflected in Matthew 6:26: "Look at the birds. They don't plant or harvest or store food in barns, for your heavenly Father feeds them. And aren't you far more valuable to him than they are?" (NLT).

Or, "So if you sinful people know how to give good gifts to your children, how much more will your heavenly Father give good gifts to those who ask him" (Matt. 7:11, NLT).

Or, "In the same way, it is not my heavenly Father's will that even one of these little ones should perish" (Matt. 18:14, NLT).

So get to know this God who is so generous that your fears will flee as you trust him with all the details of your life. Keep the phrase "the God of all comfort" in mind today, and as fear or anxiety raises its ugly head, let it flee in light of his goodness.

Prayer

Father of mercy and comfort, let your true nature soak deep into my bones. Fill my heart and mind with the knowledge of who you truly are and give me joy in the fact that you want to re-father me. Let me know your kindness and see your moment-by-moment care for me. Help me to set aside my faulty, earthly misconceptions and trust you fully with my fears.

P.M. Meditation

How did you do today? Were you able to believe that God has your best interests at heart and to trust him with the details of your life? If not, hand them over to him now and rest in the fact that he watches over you each moment, even as you sleep.

Day 12: Who Is God?

Brother

A.M. Meditation

Scripture Passage

Because God's children are human beings—made of flesh and blood—the Son also became flesh and blood. For only as a human being could he die, and only by dying could he break the power of the devil, who had the power of death. Only in this way could he set free all who have lived their lives as slaves to the fear of dying.

We also know that the Son did not come to help angels; he came to help the descendants of Abraham. Therefore, it was necessary for him to be made in every respect like us, his brothers and sisters, so that he could be our merciful and faithful High Priest before God. Then he could offer a sacrifice that would take away the sins of the people. Since he himself has gone through suffering and testing, he is able to help us when we are being tested. (Heb. 2:14–18, NLT)

Meditation

The way we know without doubt of God's loving nature is through his Son, Jesus. God sent him to break Satan's power and to "set free all who lived their lives as slaves to the fear of dying." So not only did God send his very own to demonstrate his true self, but in the process he freed us from our greatest fear, that of dying.

He became in "every respect like us, his brothers and sisters." Not only is God our Father, but he gave us Christ, who could become "family" to us. He's the perfect older brother who will never pick on us; instead he will always pave the way so that we can better handle what life throws at us.

Best of all, Jesus walked the way we walk, facing the same kinds of suffering and temptation we face. That gives us confidence in the God who literally understands what it is like to be human, including what it is like to fear. The night before his death, he begged God to "let this cup of suffering be taken away from me" (Matt. 26:39, NLT). Surely that was fear, yet he concluded, "Yet I want your will to be done, not mine." In other words, he trusted his heavenly Father with all his fears.

As you encounter fears today, let the phrase "he is able to help us" flow through your mind and give you the peace of his brotherly presence.

Prayer

Jesus, thank you for becoming a man and breaking Satan's stronghold of fear in my life. I am so grateful that you walked the path I walk and understand my deepest fears, and yet you promise me your presence and help as I face that which overwhelms me. Make me aware of your companionship today no matter what I face.

P.M. Meditation

Were you aware of God's presence today? Did you understand that Jesus was not only with you in your fears, but understood them? Rejoice in any victory you had in this way and sleep soundly in the knowledge that he is still acting on your behalf.

Day 13: Who Is God?

Trustworthy

A.M. Meditation

Scripture Passage

Now when people take an oath, they call on someone greater than themselves to hold them to it. And without any question that oath is binding. God also bound himself with an oath, so that those who received the promise could be perfectly sure that he would never change his mind. So God has given both his promise and his oath. These two things are unchangeable because it is impossible for God to lie. Therefore, we who have fled to him for refuge can have great confidence as we hold to the hope that lies before us. This hope is a strong and trustworthy anchor for our souls. It leads us through the curtain into God's inner sanctuary. Jesus has already gone in there for us. He has become our eternal High Priest in the order of Melchizedek. (Heb. 6:16–20, NLT)

Meditation

Today's passage gives us a strong and secure view of our relationship with God. This is a God we can absolutely trust, because he has promised to care for us and he would never lie. That makes him trustworthy beyond our wildest imagination.

The word pictures in this passage are some of my favorite in Scripture. The phrase "we fled to him for refuge" takes my imagination to a strong, impenetrable fortress that no enemy can scale. The security that gives me is enormous.

I also love the sentence, "This hope is a strong and trustworthy anchor for our souls." Because I emotionally bounce around like a beach ball on ocean waves, the idea of an anchor for my soul is wonderful. I can tether myself to God and the truth of his Word, knowing there is no place more secure. That hope also "leads us through the curtain into God's inner sanctuary," giving me a place to dwell where no evil can touch me.

Choose one of these word pictures to dwell on today. When you come across something that makes you feel anxious or fearful, let those thoughts convince you of God's trustworthiness.

Prayer

You are truly my refuge and the anchor of my soul. Thank you for your constant presence and steadfast faithfulness to me when I need you most. Help me to dwell today in your inner sanctuary, secure that nothing can ultimately hurt me if I am under your care.

P.M. Meditation

Were you aware that God is trustworthy no matter what fears assaulted you today? Let the knowledge of that wash over you now and clear away the failings and fears of the day. Rest in the certain hope that can carry you through any difficulty.

Day 14: Who Is God?

Wise

A.M. Meditation

Scripture Passage

"I am Joseph!" he said to his brothers. "Is my father still alive?" But his brothers were speechless! They were stunned to realize that Joseph was standing there in front of them. "Please, come closer," he said to them. So they came closer. And he said again, "I am Joseph, your brother, whom you sold into slavery in Egypt. But don't be upset, and don't be angry with yourselves for selling me to this place. It was God who sent me here ahead of you to preserve your lives. This famine that has ravaged the land for two years will last five more years, and there will be neither plowing nor harvesting. God has sent me ahead of you to keep you and your families alive and to preserve many survivors. So it was God who sent me here, not you! And he is the one who made me an adviser to Pharaoh—the manager of his entire palace and the governor of all Egypt." (Gen. 45:3–8, NLT)

Meditation

We can learn a great deal from Joseph about how to handle fear. This is the Joseph who was sold into slavery by his brothers and who faced an unjust imprisonment, since he was falsely accused of a crime he didn't commit. In this scene, he reveals his identity to his brothers, and in the process reveals to us his remarkable confidence in God's wisdom.

Surely, when Joseph was initially making the long journey to Egypt, or when he was sitting in prison, ignored by the one who promised to help get him out, he must have felt great fear. I have no doubt that at times it was overwhelming and all-consuming. He probably even felt abandoned by God, and certainly must have wondered what in the world God was doing. But by this scene, he was speaking through the lens of experience. In hindsight, he recognized that God had a plan all along and was allowing Joseph to go through each step of this journey for a reason.

So what does that mean for us and for our fears? It means that if we are seeking God, he is working—even when it seems to make no sense. Because of Joseph's example and confidence in God's wisdom, we can have the same certainty that God is working in and through us to accomplish his purposes. As a result, we can let our fears drift away as we remain rooted in God's wise counsel in our lives. We can echo Paul's words in Romans 16:27: "All glory to the only wise God, through Jesus Christ, forever. Amen." (NLT)

Today as you face your fears, let that description of God drive away Satan's nudge to panic. The "only wise God" has not abandoned you and is working to accomplish good in and through you.

Prayer

You are truly the only wise God and the only one who can see the big picture. Help me to trust you with the details of my life that often do not make sense from my perspective. Take away my fears as I lean heavily on you and depend on you to turn confusion into certainty.

P.M. Meditation

When you faced uncertainty and fear today, were you able to trust God to weave the details of your life into a finished tapestry that makes sense? If not, give those fears to him now and rest in the knowledge that he not only knows what to do but will bring you through these circumstances with power and wisdom.

Day 15: Who Is God?

Self-Sufficient

A.M. Meditation

Scripture Passage

So Paul, standing before the council, addressed them as follows: "Men of Athens, I notice that you are very religious in every way, for as I was walking along I saw your many shrines. And one of your altars had this inscription on it: 'To an Unknown God.' This God, whom you worship without knowing, is the one I'm telling you about.

"He is the God who made the world and everything in it. Since he is Lord of heaven and earth, he doesn't live in man-made temples, and human hands can't serve his needs—for he has no needs. He himself gives life and breath to everything, and he satisfies every need. From one man he created all the nations throughout the whole earth. He decided beforehand when they should rise and fall, and he determined their boundaries." (Acts 17:22–26, NLT)

Meditation

In Acts 17, we see Paul explaining who God is to those who had no prior knowledge of him. As he paints this picture, we also gain glimpses into God's nature. Through this description, we understand that God has made the world, has no needs, gives life and breath to everything, and determines nations' boundaries.

This snapshot of God helps us comprehend that he is self-sufficient. He doesn't need anyone to do anything for him and has no unmet needs. There is no dependency in him and he never fails to be in control. There is nothing he lacks and no purpose he cannot accomplish. Perhaps the best way to understand what it means that God is self-sufficient is by considering the opposite: God will never be helpless, inadequate, incompetent, insufficient, impotent, or weak.

So what does that mean for our fears? Asking that question is almost laughable in light of God's self-sufficiency. As it says in Romans 8:31b (NIV), "If God is for us, who can be against us?" If he is truly self-sufficient, nothing is beyond him. Our worries for safety, provision, courage, health, relationships, and so on dim as we trust each of those things to a God who can do anything.

As you go through your day, commit Romans 8:31b to memory and even say it aloud when you doubt or fear. The power of this truth can help dissipate your fears as the bright sun dissipates mist.

Prayer

Lord, you truly are a God who has absolutely no needs. As I face all the needs, fears, and concerns of my day, I pray that you will help me keep that in mind and to bank my security on your self-sufficiency.

P.M. Meditation

Did you keep God's self-sufficiency in mind today? Did the knowledge of that help put your fears in perspective? If not, let him assure you now and sleep well in that certainty.

Day 16: Who Is God?

All-Knowing

A.M. Meditation

Scripture Passage

O Lord, you have examined my heart

and know everything about me.

You know when I sit down or stand up.

You know my thoughts even when I'm far away.

You see me when I travel

and when I rest at home.

You know everything I do.

You know what I am going to say

even before I say it, Lord.

You go before me and follow me.

You place your hand of blessing on my head.

Such knowledge is too wonderful for me,

too great for me to understand! (Ps. 139:1–6, NLT)

Meditation

Most who grew up in Christian homes learned from their earliest days that God sees everything. Psalm 139 points out the many things he knows: my heart, everything about me, where I am and what I'm doing, my thoughts, and my words. Other parts of Scripture talk about how God sees the whole earth (2 Chron. 16:9), knows our needs (Matt. 6:32), and even knows the future (Isa. 46:9–10).

As we mentioned before, many of us have seen the fact that God knows everything as a negative thing, but if we feel that way, we are not convinced of his unconditional love for us. Being aware that he is all-loving makes the fact that he is all-knowing a wonderful thing. We can trust that he knows what has happened to us, what is happening to us, and what will happen to us—all wrapped in the fact that he loves us perfectly.

What does that mean for our fears? They are blown away like the seeds of a dandelion in a strong wind. They disappear as we rest in the fact that no matter what we have to face, God is there with us, understands what we are going through, and will never abandon us. And he will always act out of wisdom.

So today, as you face things you fear or that make you feel anxious, think *God, you know everything* . . . and then trust that he will carry you through this fear with grace and wisdom.

Prayer

Father, thank you that nothing takes you by surprise. You are never startled or taken off-guard. You always know what is going to happen and you surround that knowledge with your love and care. Keep that close to my heart and mind today.

P.M. Meditation

As you faced fears and anxieties today, were you aware that God has already taken everything into account and acted in his wisdom? If not, think through that now and sleep soundly tonight, assured that he knows all.

Day 17: Who Is God?

All-Powerful

A.M. Meditation

Scripture Passage

"Where were you when I laid the earth's foundation?

   Tell me, if you understand.

Who marked off its dimensions? Surely you know!

   Who stretched a measuring line across it?

On what were its footings set,

   or who laid its cornerstone—

while the morning stars sang together

   and all the angels shouted for joy?

Who shut up the sea behind doors

when it burst forth from the womb,

when I made the clouds its garment

and wrapped it in thick darkness,

when I fixed limits for it

and set its doors and bars in place,

when I said, 'This far you may come and no farther;

here is where your proud waves halt'?" (Job 38:4–11, NIV)

Meditation

It was hard for me to narrow down the verses from Job to use in today's Scripture reading. I remember reading Job 38–41 as a new Christian and being humbled and in awe of God's power and might as described in those chapters. If you have time, read all four chapters to get the full impact of this astounding account of the many things God did and does. If you are like me, it will give you chills each time you read it.

The fact that God is all-powerful pretty well squashes any fear, anxiety, or worry. A God who laid the earth's foundations and shut up the sea where it should go is big enough to handle anything that could cause me consternation. Couple that with the fact that he is always good, and we have a marriage of two intertwined, unbeatable qualities that cause all fears to flee.

Psalm 147:5 says, "Great is our Lord and mighty in power . . ." (NIV). Memorize that phrase and say it each time fear or worry threatens you today.

Prayer

What a mighty, powerful God you are! Fill my heart and mind today with the knowledge of your dominion and sovereignty over all things. Let me dwell in the security of knowing that you have all circumstances under your control.

P.M. Meditation

Did you keep perspective today, knowing that God can do anything? Were you able to set your fears aside with that assurance? If not, take time to do that now. Give him each thing that causes you anxiety and rest in him.

Day 18: Who Is God?

Just

A.M. Meditation

Scripture Passage

We ought always to thank God for you, brothers and sisters, and rightly so, because your faith is growing more and more, and the love all of you have for one another is increasing. Therefore, among God's churches we boast about your perseverance and faith in all the persecutions and trials you are enduring.

All this is evidence that God's judgment is right, and as a result you will be counted worthy of the kingdom of God, for which you are suffering. God is just: He will pay back trouble to those who trouble you and give relief to you who are troubled, and to us as well. This will happen when the Lord Jesus is revealed from heaven in blazing fire with his powerful angels. (2 Thess. 1:3–7, NIV)

No worries - justice will come - in the meantime see enemies as a mission field & not enemies!

Meditation

Paul wrote to the Thessalonians to encourage them that although they were suffering persecution, they could be assured that God is just and will not let such injustice go unpunished.

Such reassurances may not ring true with us if we don't feel we are being persecuted. Talk of justice rings louder and more desperately among people who feel they are not finding it. That's why Martin Luther King Jr. spoke so passionately about justice, since his people were not receiving it.

But think what these verses might mean to a Christian in a Muslim nation or in a country ruled with the iron fist of a dictator. That person would find this passage comforting beyond measure, and would long for the day the "Lord Jesus is revealed from heaven in blazing fire with his powerful angels."

So how does the fact that God is just allay our fears? We are reassured that he will never abuse power; he will never act selfishly or arbitrarily, but always with purpose and out of love. We do not have to fear anything the world throws at us because Jesus will make everything right.

As you go about your day, keep in mind one of these phrases: "God's judgment is right" and/or "God is just." When you feel life is unfair or you fear your future will be unfair, rest in the knowledge that all things will be made right in God's time and way.

Prayer

Lord Jesus, we long for the day you will come and make all things right. We know there will be all sorts of inequities and unfairness in the meantime, yet you are not only aware of them but anxious to correct them. Come, Lord Jesus!

P.M. Meditation

When things seemed unfair today, were you able to put it in
perspective? If not, read today's passage again and sleep peacefully in
the knowledge that God will right all wrongs.

Day 19: Who Is God?

Never Changing

A.M. Meditation

Scripture Passage

Long ago you laid the foundation of the earth

   and made the heavens with your hands.

They will perish, but you remain forever;

   they will wear out like old clothing.

You will change them like a garment

   and discard them.

But you are always the same;

   you will live forever.

The children of your people

will live in security.

Their children's children

will thrive in your presence. (Ps. 102:25–28, NLT)

Meditation

As solid as our planet seems, it will pass away. This may have been a startling statement to those who heard it when the psalmist penned these words almost 3,000 years ago. Today, with an inundation of apocalyptic novels and movies, we seem to accept this as fact, and only debate how it will come about.

The end of the earth is treated as casually as a change of clothes in this passage—however, as depressing as this information is, the psalmist goes on to say of God, "But you are always the same; you will live forever."

The fact that God never changes is particularly important concerning his purposes and his promises. He will never be thwarted in his plans or tempted to break his promises. He can be counted on.

And what does God's immutability do concerning our fear? It crushes it as we realize that God will never break the promises he has given us throughout the Scriptures, nor will he abandon his plans for us and for the world. As our passage concludes, "The children of your people will live in security. Their children's children will thrive in your presence."

As you go about your day, remember the words "you remain forever" and rest secure in the fact that you are connected to such a powerful and unshakeable being.

Prayer

Lord, I am in awe of you since you not only made the heavens and the earth but will outlast them for all of eternity. Thank you that I can count on you to never change your promises or your purposes. That allows me to release my fears to your charge and care.

P.M. Meditation

How did your day go? Did you experience wonderful victory or complete disaster? If the former, praise God for his help. If the latter, ask him to help you trust him more fully tomorrow.

Day 20: Who Is God?

Merciful

A.M. Meditation

Scripture Passage

Show me the right path, O Lord;

    point out the road for me to follow.

Lead me by your truth and teach me,

    for you are the God who saves me.

    All day long I put my hope in you.

Remember, O Lord, your compassion and unfailing love,

    which you have shown from long ages past.

Do not remember the rebellious sins of my youth.

    Remember me in the light of your unfailing love,

for you are merciful, O Lord. (Ps. 25:4–7, NLT)

Meditation

Mercy is not a word we in the Western world think much about these days. We are used to people giving us the benefit of the doubt, and even if we are proven guilty, we assume that the punishment will not be so great. But do we think the same in relation to God? If we've done something we know is wrong, are we so scared of God's response that we don't know how to be honest with him? Do we vainly try to hide the information from him by not talking it over with him, or do we admit he knows it all but feel so overwhelmed by our consciences that we assume God has utterly rejected us?

According to today's passage, we should instead bask in the glow of God's great love and acceptance in spite of our sin. He opens his arms wide and welcomes us into his presence with joy—and with merciful forgiveness.

As you face your fears today, let the words "All day long I put my hope in you" fill your heart and mind.

Prayer

Heavenly Father, you truly are loving, compassionate, and merciful. I should never fear being perfectly open and honest with you. Fill me with confidence in your willingness to accept me, even with all my flaws, and take away any semblance of fear that threatens my relationship with you.

P.M. Meditation

Is guilt weighing you down? If so, confess it now and know that God is merciful and is delighted to forgive you, no matter what the sin. Now rest well in the sweetness of that mercy.

Day 21: Who Is God?

Gracious

A.M. Meditation

Scripture Passage

"But they, our ancestors, became arrogant and stiff-necked, and they did not obey your commands. They refused to listen and failed to remember the miracles you performed among them. They became stiff-necked and in their rebellion appointed a leader in order to return to their slavery. But you are a forgiving God, gracious and compassionate, slow to anger and abounding in love. Therefore you did not desert them, even when they cast for themselves an image of a calf and said, 'This is your god, who brought you up out of Egypt,' or when they committed awful blasphemies.

"Because of your great compassion you did not abandon them in the wilderness. By day the pillar of cloud did not fail to guide them on their path, nor the pillar of fire by night to shine on the way they were to take. You gave your good Spirit to instruct them. You did not withhold your manna from their mouths, and you gave them water for their thirst. For forty years you sustained them in the wilderness; they lacked nothing, their clothes did not wear out nor did their feet become swollen. (Neh. 9:16–21, NIV)

Meditation

God gives us a clear picture of how gracious he is in how he dealt with the Hebrews when he led them out of Egypt. In spite of his miraculous deliverance, they refused to trust him and even wanted to return to slavery in Egypt.

Even though he cared for them by providing food and clothing, as well as his Spirit to guide them—literally (isn't that what we all long for?)—they not only refused to trust him, but created another "god" to worship, giving that make-believe god the credit for all the LORD had done. Nevertheless, God was "forgiving . . . gracious and compassionate, slow to anger and abounding in love."

The great news for us is that if God was so patient and gracious with a group of people who utterly abandoned him, he will be even more gracious with us as we try to follow him but occasionally fail in our efforts. It also means that our fears and anxieties will dissipate like water poured onto hot desert sand. We can be confident that God will give us as many chances as we need to get it right. He will never ignore our efforts or refuse to meet us in our helplessness.

So as you battle your anxieties today, keep in mind that God is "gracious and compassionate." Let those two attributes of God chase away any fears that attack you, and stand firm in his love.

Prayer

Thank you for being gracious, O God. I am grateful that I never need fear that you will be impatient with me or refuse to help me when I ask.

Your divine grace is beyond human comprehension, and you have said that you will help me when I call. I ask for that assistance today.

P.M. Meditation

Were you able to keep in mind that God is gracious and compassionate? If so, how did that help you with your fears and anxiety? Dwell on that now and rest well in the comfort and knowledge of that truth.

Day 22: Who Is God?

Spirit

A.M. Meditation

Scripture Passage

[Jesus said,] "If you love me, keep my commands. And I will ask the Father, and he will give you another advocate to help you and be with you forever—the Spirit of truth. The world cannot accept him, because it neither sees him nor knows him. But you know him, for he lives with you and will be in you. I will not leave you as orphans; I will come to you. Before long, the world will not see me anymore, but you will see me. Because I live, you also will live. On that day you will realize that I am in my Father, and you are in me, and I am in you. Whoever has my commands and keeps them is the one who loves me. The one who loves me will be loved by my Father, and I too will love them and show myself to them." (John 14:15–21, NIV)

Meditation

At this point in the Gospel of John, Jesus reassures his disciples that he is not abandoning them. As he encourages them, he also buoys our hearts with the wonderful assurance, "I will not leave you as orphans." How is he making sure they, and we, are not left alone? His Father is sending the Spirit of truth to be with all believers. This passage gives us a wonderful picture of how intertwined, yet uniquely individual, is each person of the Trinity.

It also reinforces what Jesus said earlier, in John 4:24 (NIV): "God is spirit, and his worshipers must worship in the Spirit and in truth." Because God is spirit, he can accompany and guide us in a way that a merely physical being could not. He can walk with us through our fears and help us face our anxious thoughts. According to this passage, he will help us obey his commands, obedience which is inseparable from our love for him. This reassures us that no matter what troubles us, he will help us gain perspective and victory.

Today, commit to memory the phrase "he lives with [me]." Then, as you face whatever terrifies you—or what merely increases your heart rate—be confident that the mighty God who created and rules the universe is dwelling in you through his Holy Spirit.

Prayer

I am bowled over by the fact that you not only love me, but that you give your Holy Spirit to walk with me each day. Thank you for the reassurance that "If God is for us, who can be against us?" (Rom. 8:31b, NIV). I bank my emotional well-being and my very life on that today.

P.M. Meditation

Were you aware of God's presence with you today? Were you confident that he not only loves you but literally walked with you throughout the day? If you forgot, think about it now and sleep peacefully in the knowledge of his presence.

Day 23: Who Is God?

Awesome

A.M. Meditation

Scripture Passage

"Listen to this, Job;

stop and consider God's wonders.

Do you know how God controls the clouds

and makes his lightning flash?

Do you know how the clouds hang poised,

those wonders of him who has perfect knowledge?

You who swelter in your clothes

when the land lies hushed under the south wind,

can you join him in spreading out the skies,

hard as a mirror of cast bronze?

"Tell us what we should say to him;

we cannot draw up our case because of our darkness.

Should he be told that I want to speak?

Would anyone ask to be swallowed up?

Now no one can look at the sun,

bright as it is in the skies

after the wind has swept them clean.

Out of the north he comes in golden splendor;

God comes in awesome majesty.

The Almighty is beyond our reach and exalted in power;

in his justice and great righteousness, he does not oppress.

Therefore, people revere him,

for does he not have regard for all the wise in heart?" (Job 37:14–24, NIV)

Meditation

As I mentioned before, the last few chapters of Job are some of my favorite passages in the Bible. There are few parts of Scripture that demonstrate so clearly how awesome God is.

Today we use the word *awesome* so casually it has lost its meaning. I remember when we took our son to see the mountains for the first time. He often talked about how awesome things were, but when he saw the Rockies, he amended all previous times he'd used the word and declared, "This is awesome. Nothing I earlier said was awesome really is."

That is similar to the way I feel when the power and majesty of God truly get through to me. I understand that he is awesome in a way that nothing and no one else has ever truly been.

The writer of our passage compares how awesome God is to what it is like to look at the sun. We all know it's so bright we can't look at it for very long. As it says, "The Almighty is beyond our reach and exalted in power."

So what does this have to do with our fear? It means anything we are afraid of is so diminished and powerless in comparison to God that it is completely impotent. Nothing can stand against God's awesomeness.

When you encounter something you are afraid of today, remember that "God comes in awesome majesty" and rest in confidence that nothing can defeat him. You are safe in his care.

Prayer

Father, I thank you that you define the word *awesome* and that everything else pales in comparison to you. Help me to remember that you come in awesome majesty on my behalf. You are my friend, not my enemy, so all my fears can be chased away in your presence.

P.M. Meditation

Were you able to remember that "God comes in awesome majesty" as you faced that which you fear today? If not, think about this as you wind down your day and rest easily in the knowledge that you have nothing to fear with such a God.

Day 24: Who Is God?

Holy

A.M. Meditation

Scripture Passage

"You must faithfully keep all my commands by putting them into practice, for I am the LORD. Do not bring shame on my holy name, for I will display my holiness among the people of Israel. I am the LORD who makes you holy. It was I who rescued you from the land of Egypt, that I might be your God. I am the LORD." (Lev. 22:31–33, NLT)

Meditation

Our passage is inadequate in emphasizing God's holiness. If we read all of Exodus and Leviticus, we might get a glimpse of how holy he is. The many laws and commands that are laid out in these two books are to help Israel (and us) understand that God is holy and that his followers are to be holy too.

Many of the attributes of God we have been covering can be compared to similar attributes we see and understand in some people, but holiness cannot be understood in human terms at all. Nothing is holy besides God, and nothing can make us holy besides God.

Our fears and anxieties become particularly ridiculous in light of God's holiness. As we immerse ourselves in him, we are surrounded and protected by his holiness. He is otherworldly and above the fray that causes us angst. Nothing can shake or thwart him. Three times in our passage, God states emphatically, "I am the LORD." Clearly, this is something he wants us to know and to stake our lives upon.

So, as you go about your day, keep the phrase "I am the LORD" firmly in your thoughts. When you recognize a fear or anxiety, toss it to the Lord with confidence that he is so above that fear that it becomes insignificant in comparison.

Prayer

Holy God, I thank you that you are above everything that causes me to fear. You are much greater than that which is causing me anxiety. Help me to keep that confidence throughout my day and to remember who you truly are.

P.M. Meditation

Were you able to keep God's holiness at the forefront of your thoughts today? Did it help? If not, have you forgotten that God's perfect holiness is tempered by his perfect love? Let all your fears melt away in that knowledge.

Day 25: Who Is God?

Provider

A.M. Meditation

Scripture Passage

"No one can serve two masters. For you will hate one and love the other; you will be devoted to one and despise the other. You cannot serve both God and money.

"That is why I tell you not to worry about everyday life—whether you have enough food and drink, or enough clothes to wear. Isn't life more than food, and your body more than clothing? Look at the birds. They don't plant or harvest or store food in barns, for your heavenly Father feeds them. And aren't you far more valuable to him than they are? Can all your worries add a single moment to your life?

"And why worry about your clothing? Look at the lilies of the field and how they grow. They don't work or make their clothing, yet Solomon in all his glory was not dressed as beautifully as they are. And if God cares so wonderfully for wildflowers that are here today and thrown into the fire tomorrow, he will certainly care for you. Why do you have so little faith?

"So don't worry about these things, saying, 'What will we eat? What will we drink? What will we wear?' These things dominate the thoughts of unbelievers, but your heavenly Father already knows all your needs. Seek the Kingdom of God above all else, and live righteously, and he will give you everything you need.

"So don't worry about tomorrow, for tomorrow will bring its own worries. Today's trouble is enough for today." (Matt. 6:24–34, NLT)

Meditation

So many of our worries are tied to money. We live in a complicated society and our financial obligations can be overwhelming at times. It's easy to read today's passage and think, *But I need so much more than food and clothes. I need insurance, dental care, housing, entertainment, phones, computers,* and so on and so on. But our passage also says, "he will give you everything you need."

The trouble is, it's easy to confuse needs with wants in our day and age. Because we see others who have more than we do, it's easy to feel we are being left out and require more than we actually do to live well.

But whether you have a lot or a little is beside the point. The point is that God is the one who provides, and we can trust him to give us what we need. I've had many times in life when I wanted to be free from financial worries, and so dreamed of inheriting a fortune from a distant relative I didn't know or winning the lottery, even if I didn't buy a ticket. But God has not supplied for me that way. Instead, he wants me to learn that everything is from his hand and that he will take care of me. The more I trust him to do that, the more my worries flee. He is a good father and will not let us down.

As you go through your day, remember that "he will give you everything you need" and live in that security.

Prayer

Father, help me to trust you even when I don't see a way. You have promised to give me everything I need, so if I don't have something, I trust I don't need it. Help me to trust you, not money or things.

P.M. Meditation

Were you able to trust God with all the details of your life today? Even the things that seem to be lacking? If you felt anxious about things today, admit that to God now, and ask him to care for you by providing your true needs and to help you let go of what is not a true need.

Day 26: Who Is God?

Transcendent

A.M. Meditation

Scripture Passage

Who else has held the oceans in his hand?

   Who has measured off the heavens with his fingers?

Who else knows the weight of the earth

   or has weighed the mountains and hills on a scale?

Who is able to advise the Spirit of the Lord?

   Who knows enough to give him advice or teach him?

Has the Lord ever needed anyone's advice?

   Does he need instruction about what is good?

Did someone teach him what is right

or show him the path of justice?

No, for all the nations of the world

are but a drop in the bucket.

They are nothing more

than dust on the scales.

He picks up the whole earth

as though it were a grain of sand. (Isa. 40:12–15, NLT)

Meditation

Transcendent is not a word we use very often (perhaps you've never used it). I have occasionally used it to describe an experience that was so astounding that it took my breath away. For example, when we went to the upper tundra area of the Rocky Mountains, I understood why the Native Americans thought it was a holy place. Just being there was an experience I could describe in no other way than *transcendent*.

The Merriam-Webster Dictionary defines transcendence as "extending or lying beyond the limits of ordinary experience." My experience in the Rockies was such an occurrence; it pulled me into feeling something I'd never felt before. However, when we speak of God being transcendent, it goes beyond this. He is, by definition, beyond the limits of ordinary experience. As today's passage says, "Who else has held the oceans in his hand? Who has measured off the heavens with his fingers?"

What does that mean for our fears? It means that no matter what we fear, we trust a God who is above and beyond anything life can throw at us. He's above the fray and completely unaffected by it. As our passage says, "Did someone teach him what is right or show him the path of justice?"

God knows what you fear and has already made plans to make it right. He will not ultimately falter or be thwarted in any way, because he is transcendent. As you go about your day, keep the phrase "Who else knows . . . ?" in mind each time you come up against something that is beyond your ability to handle. Realize that there is no one else like the Lord who knows and has power over all things.

Prayer

Father God, help me to realize how truly different you are from any other person I've experienced in life. I know that you have none of the flaws we humans have and that you are all-wise and powerful. Help me to rest in that today as I trust you with my anxiety.

P.M. Meditation

Were you able to keep in mind that God is over and above all things? Did the knowledge of his transcendence help you conquer your fears and anxieties? If not, give them to him now and take time to simply dwell on ways that God is better than any human you've ever known.

Day 27: Who Is God?

Healer

A.M. Meditation

Scripture Passage

Bless the Lord, O my soul,

  and all that is within me,

  bless his holy name!

Bless the Lord, O my soul,

  and forget not all his benefits,

who forgives all your iniquity,

  who heals all your diseases,

who redeems your life from the pit,

  who crowns you with steadfast love and mercy,

who satisfies you with good

so that your youth is renewed like the eagle's. (Ps. 103:1–5, ESV)

Meditation

What does the fact that God is healer have to do with our fears? Plenty! Most of us have fears about our health and well-being. We want to feel good, so when illness or injury threaten, we feel anxious. Some of this anxiety is good and God-given. For example, if you feel your hand getting too hot as you hold it over an open fire, you should pull it back. Or if you eat a dozen donuts a day, your fear of developing health problems is valid. If you regularly pass every other car on the road, the anxiety you feel about getting into an accident is not far-fetched.

But what about the anxieties that come when your behavior has done nothing to lead to trouble? What if you received a cancer diagnosis or were in an accident when you were doing everything in your power to avoid those things?   Whether you feel your behavior led to your current problems or not, your fears can be allayed by knowing that God is the ultimate healer. Yet, clearly not everyone is healed. So what did the psalmist mean when he said God "heals all your diseases"?

One way to look at it is that God does eventually heal us. As a friend of mine who is battling cancer for the second time says, "I know I will be healed ultimately when I go to heaven." Also, most of the time God does heal us here on earth. Think of all the illnesses or accidents you've recovered from throughout your lifetime. There are probably more of them than you can count. Generally, God heals. So if you now have a more serious disease, you should assume that God is going to heal you. And even if he does not, you can follow the lead of the psalmist and say, "Bless the Lord, O my soul." Or as it says in the New Living Translation, "Let all that I am praise the Lord."

Keep that phrase in mind as you go about your day, and let it fill your thoughts when the fear of disease or bodily harm haunts you.

Prayer

Thank you, God, that you are the ultimate healer. Let all my fear fade away in that knowledge. Help me to be filled with your praises and to trust you completely instead of fearing what might happen to me. I want you, not my illness, to be my focus. Help me in this. I can't do it alone.

P.M. Meditation

Are you able to rest in the fact that God is your ultimate healer? If that is still a struggle, end your day by letting the words "Bless the Lord, O my soul" flow through your heart and mind.

Day 28: Who Is God?

Victorious

A.M. Meditation

Scripture Passage

Jesus asked, "Do you finally believe? But the time is coming—indeed it's here now—when you will be scattered, each one going his own way, leaving me alone. Yet I am not alone because the Father is with me. I have told you all this so that you may have peace in me. Here on earth you will have many trials and sorrows. But take heart, because I have overcome the world."

After saying all these things, Jesus looked up to heaven and said, "Father, the hour has come. Glorify your Son so he can give glory back to you. For you have given him authority over everyone. He gives eternal life to each one you have given him. And this is the way to have eternal life—to know you, the only true God, and Jesus Christ, the one you sent to earth. I brought glory to you here on earth by completing the work you gave me to do. Now, Father, bring me into the glory we shared before the world began." (John 16:31–17:5, NLT)

Meditation

"Here on earth you will have many trials and sorrows. But take heart, because I have overcome the world." Have more reassuring words ever been written? No matter what we are facing, we have the wonderful certainty that Jesus Christ, who loved us enough to die for us, has complete authority over the world. He will gain the final victory and all our problems will pale in comparison to his glory.

As we face our fears, this, above all else, will chase away our anxiety. We are aligned with one who cannot lose. He alone has the final say, and when he says, "Enough!" all will be made right. When we despair of all the world is throwing at us, we can be confident in Jesus' indomitable kingdom that will not, cannot, lose.

So no matter what anxieties, worries, or fears assault you today, set them aside with confidence because of this great truth. When you feel your anxiety rising, repeat the phrase "I have overcome the world" and let the power of those words—or better yet, the power of the one who said those words—take away any worry or fear that is trying to gain victory over you. It seems like such a fierce battle, but someday we'll see it as a mere skirmish in the larger scheme of things. Jesus wins.

Prayer

Jesus, it is so reassuring that you have already told us the end of the story. You cannot lose, so Satan, the world, and fleshly failures hold no power over me. I am so grateful. Let me not forget it for a moment.

P.M. Meditation

Were you able to remember that Jesus has overcome the world? He doesn't say that he will someday find a way to overcome the world, but that he has already overcome the world. He has a plan that is perfect, and we can trust him. Rest in that truth tonight.

Day 29: Who Is God?

Angry

A.M. Meditation

Scripture Passage

They come together to spy on me—

    watching my every step, eager to kill me.

Don't let them get away with their wickedness;

    in your anger, O God, bring them down.

You keep track of all my sorrows.

    You have collected all my tears in your bottle.

    You have recorded each one in your book.

My enemies will retreat when I call to you for help.

    This I know: God is on my side!

I praise God for what he has promised;

yes, I praise the Lord for what he has promised.

I trust in God, so why should I be afraid?

What can mere mortals do to me? (Ps. 56:6–11, NLT)

Meditation

I struggled with whether to talk about God's anger or God as judge. I chose the former because there are so many passages about God's anger, I felt it would be remiss to ignore them.

We shy away from passages about God's anger because we have had bad experiences with people's anger. I imagine most of us have trouble thinking of anyone whose anger was a positive thing. Instead, we often see it as something unjust that we didn't deserve. Or we think of it as someone being out of control and using his or her anger as a weapon to annihilate those around them.

This couldn't be further from the truth of God's anger. All human illustrations fall short; the closest we can get to understanding it is the righteous anger we hear in a speech by Martin Luther King, Jr., or the fury of a father whose daughter was captured and abused by a terrorist organization. These examples give us a glimpse of anger as it should be, but it is still imperfect because all human anger is tainted by sin. We cannot separate who we are from how we feel.

That is not true of God. He is not a slave to his own emotions as we are. Even when we are angry for all the right reasons, we have to question our fury because it so easily runs away with us and becomes our master. This can never happen to God. He is master of all, never mastered by anything.

So what does this mean for our fears? It reassures us that God has our back. He knows what threatens us and his anger burns against all evil. And as our psalmist concludes, "I trust in God, so why should I be afraid? What can mere mortals do to me?"

Prayer

God, I thank you for your anger, because it is perfect and never meted out unfairly. I pray you would help me to know your anger is not against me, since you see Christ's perfection rather than my sins. That means your anger is only against those in rebellion against you. Because of that, I rest in your love and protection, secure in you. Help me to keep the question "What can mere mortals do to me?" firmly in my thoughts today.

P.M. Meditation

Did you think about God's anger as a positive, rather than a negative, thing today? If not, dwell on that now and rest well in the knowledge that he has your back and loves you perfectly no matter what.

Day 30: Who Is God?

Comforter

A.M. Meditation

Scripture Passage

All praise to God, the Father of our Lord Jesus Christ. God is our merciful Father and the source of all comfort. He comforts us in all our troubles so that we can comfort others. When they are troubled, we will be able to give them the same comfort God has given us. For the more we suffer for Christ, the more God will shower us with his comfort through Christ. (2 Cor. 1:3–5, NLT)

Meditation

What an encouraging passage, and what a good glimpse of who God is. He is "our merciful Father and the source of all comfort." And "the more we suffer for Christ, the more God will shower us with his comfort through Christ."

So what does that mean for our fears, worries, and anxieties? It means that no matter what happens to us, we know that in allowing it, God is merciful. He's not vindictive or harsh, but gentle and kind. We also know that he is there to comfort us when we face hard things.

I love how Eugene Peterson puts Isaiah 51:12 and following in *The Message*: "I, I'm the One comforting you. What are you afraid of—or who? Some man or woman who'll soon be dead? Some poor wretch destined for dust? You've forgotten me, God, who made you, who unfurled the skies, who founded the earth. And here you are, quaking like an aspen before the tantrums of a tyrant who thinks he can kick down the world."

Keep the first part of that in mind as you go about your daily tasks: "I'm the One comforting you." And let God do just that—no matter what you face.

Prayer

Thank you that you are my perfect Father. You will never be harsh or unfair. You will never make me pay the full penalty of my sins, but will always show mercy. Your arms are open wide, waiting to comfort me. Help me to recognize that as I go through this day.

P.M. Meditation

Did you keep in mind that God is your perfect Father, waiting to comfort you if you just come to him? Rest in that knowledge and certainty now as you wind down your day.

Day 31: Who Is God?

Blesser

A.M. Meditation

Scripture Passage

When Jesus saw his ministry drawing huge crowds, he climbed a hillside. Those who were apprenticed to him, the committed, climbed with him. Arriving at a quiet place, he sat down and taught his climbing companions. This is what he said:

"You're blessed when you're at the end of your rope. With less of you there is more of God and his rule.

"You're blessed when you feel you've lost what is most dear to you. Only then can you be embraced by the One most dear to you.

"You're blessed when you're content with just who you are—no more, no less. That's the moment you find yourselves proud owners of everything that can't be bought.

"You're blessed when you've worked up a good appetite for God.

He's food and drink in the best meal you'll ever eat.

"You're blessed when you care. At the moment of being 'care-full,' you find yourselves cared for.

"You're blessed when you get your inside world—your mind and heart—put right. Then you can see God in the outside world.

"You're blessed when you can show people how to cooperate instead of compete or fight. That's when you discover who you really are, and your place in God's family.

"You're blessed when your commitment to God provokes persecution. The persecution drives you even deeper into God's kingdom.

"Not only that—count yourselves blessed every time people put you down or throw you out or speak lies about you to discredit me. What it means is that the truth is too close for comfort and they are uncomfortable. You can be glad when that happens—give a cheer, even!—for though they don't like it, I do! And all heaven applauds. And know that you are in good company. My prophets and witnesses have always gotten into this kind of trouble." (Matt. 5:1–12, MSG)

Meditation

This is one of my favorite Scripture passages. It's certainly not what comes to mind when I think of being blessed or when I pray for others to be blessed. Remember all those childhood prayers, "Bless Mommy, Daddy, and Auntie Sue"? We had no idea what we were asking! We were actually saying, "Let them be poor in spirit, mourning, meek, hungering and thirsting for righteousness, merciful, pure, peacemakers, and persecuted."

So how could such things lead to happiness? Only the One who made us knows what will truly make us happy and give us satisfaction in life. We have to get to the end of ourselves and the beginning of God to gain any lasting contentment in life. And that can happen only through divine revelation and transformation, through God's Word and the Holy Spirit dwelling in us. It's the "pearl of great value" (Matt. 13:46) worth selling everything for. And ultimately, it's the secret to true satisfaction.

As you recognize your fears today, keep in mind what it means to be truly blessed. When you come up against dark thoughts and feelings of anxiety, tell yourself (and Satan), "I am blessed." That simple thought and recognition of the truth can turn things around.

Prayer

You are the blesser of my soul. You turn things upside down and give me victory when it's least expected. Help me to remember that you are always waiting to fill my heart with the awareness of your presence, the best blessing I could possible have.

P.M. Meditation

Did you keep in mind that God is constantly blessing you with his presence and goodness? Let your thoughts this evening drift to all the ways God has met you during your lifetime, and rest in him as you praise him for his goodness to you.

Day 32: Who Is God?

Head of All

A.M. Meditation

Scripture Passage

The Lord reigns, let the earth be glad;

  let the distant shores rejoice.

Clouds and thick darkness surround him;

  righteousness and justice are the foundation of his throne.

Fire goes before him

  and consumes his foes on every side.

His lightning lights up the world;

  the earth sees and trembles.

The mountains melt like wax before the Lord,

before the Lord of all the earth.

The heavens proclaim his righteousness,

and all peoples see his glory. (Ps. 97:1–6, NIV)

Meditation

We've discussed the fact that God is head of all in many different ways throughout the last month, but we can never emphasize it enough. So many of our fears are brought into perspective through our understanding of this. Although the description of God's power sounds a bit frightening in this passage, it also explains how we should feel about God's rule of all. Phrases like "let the earth be glad" give us a glimpse into what our attitude toward his power should be.

The reason we don't need to be afraid of God's awesome power is because he is on our side. He will always come to our defense and act on our behalf.

That doesn't mean that bad things will never happen to us, but it does mean that whoever perpetrated that bad thing has far more to fear than we do! God is the ultimate "big brother," a protector who has our backs.

So we can let our fears drift away in the knowledge that nothing is out of his control. Nothing escapes his notice or takes him by surprise. In general, we can relax in the certainty that nothing can touch us without his permission.

Prayer

Help me to keep in mind that you are "Lord of all the earth." As I face things that cause me to fear or feel anxious, let me rest in the confidence that you are in charge and that nothing gets past you. If the "mountains melt like wax" before you, then there is not a single thing on earth that can threaten me.

P.M. Meditation

Is it getting any easier to remember that God is in control of all things? Does this truth help you keep your fear and anxiety in perspective? Meditate on the Scripture passage we read this morning as you relax in God's love and care.

Day 33: Who Is God?

Jealous

A.M. Meditation

Scripture Passage

The Lord replied [to Moses], "Listen, I am making a covenant with you in the presence of all your people. I will perform miracles that have never been performed anywhere in all the earth or in any nation. And all the people around you will see the power of the Lord—the awesome power I will display for you. But listen carefully to everything I command you today. Then I will go ahead of you and drive out the Amorites, Canaanites, Hittites, Perizzites, Hivites, and Jebusites.

"Be very careful never to make a treaty with the people who live in the land where you are going. If you do, you will follow their evil ways and be trapped. Instead, you must break down their pagan altars, smash their sacred pillars, and cut down their Asherah poles. You must worship no other gods, for the Lord, whose very name is Jealous, is a God who is jealous about his relationship with you.

"You must not make a treaty of any kind with the people living in the land. They lust after their gods, offering sacrifices to them. They will invite you to join them in their sacrificial meals, and you will go with them. Then you will accept their daughters, who sacrifice to other gods, as wives for your sons. And they will seduce your sons to commit adultery against me by worshiping other gods. You must not make any gods of molten metal for yourselves." (Ex. 34:10–17, NLT)

Meditation

It's hard to think about God being jealous, because we see jealousy as a negative thing. We hate jealousy in ourselves as we see the way it tears us apart internally. We hate it in those we love because we feel smothered and controlled by their jealousy. This is another of those traits that only God can manifest correctly. As we've mentioned, God is not just a bigger version of ourselves—he is completely and utterly different from us since he has no propensity to sin.

Our passage today helps illustrate that. When I am jealous of another person, it's because I somehow feel inadequate. Either I compare myself to someone, or I feel threatened by someone's relationship with another. God is not in any way inadequate. Rather, he is completely self-sufficient and has no lack or need. God is jealous not because he fears he is not measuring up, but because he knows that without him we are rudderless and headed for darkness and destruction.

That was his concern for the nation of Israel in this passage. If they simply settled in with the godless cultures around them, they would soon adopt the horrendous customs those people practiced, such as child sacrifice, temple prostitution, and brutal slavery. They would drift farther and farther from God, who is the only light in this world and the only hope we have for anything good in life and for all eternity.

So what does this mean for our fears? Won't it just exacerbate them, since we know we are falling short of God's expectations? Absolutely not, because God's jealousy reaffirms his great and powerful love for us. He doesn't want to share us with other gods because he knows they are false gods who will destroy us. He knows that following anyone other than him leads to unhappiness and sorrow. By his jealousy he wants to spare us from that.

Keep the phrase "God . . . is jealous about his relationship with me" in your thoughts today. When worry and fear threaten, reflect on how he wants you to run to him for shelter and trust him to protect and care for you.

Prayer

Thank you, Lord, for being jealous for my affections. Thank you for the certainty that I can only find happiness in you. Fill my heart and mind with that confidence as I encounter things that frighten me today. Help me to know without a shadow of a doubt that you are the only safe place for me.

P.M. Meditation

Were you able to get a handle on the fact that God's jealousy for you is a good thing? That he only ever wants good for you and that being in his presence is the safest place in the world? If not, reflect on that now and rest easy tonight.

Day 34: Who Is God?

Tender

A.M. Meditation

Scripture Passage

[Zechariah's prophecy at John the Baptist's birth]:

"Praise the Lord, the God of Israel,

    because he has visited and redeemed his people.

He has sent us a mighty Savior

    from the royal line of his servant David,

just as he promised

    through his holy prophets long ago.

Now we will be saved from our enemies

and from all who hate us.

He has been merciful to our ancestors

by remembering his sacred covenant—

the covenant he swore with an oath

to our ancestor Abraham.

We have been rescued from our enemies

so we can serve God without fear,

in holiness and righteousness

for as long as we live.

And you, my little son,

will be called the prophet of the Most High,

because you will prepare the way for the Lord.

You will tell his people how to find salvation

through forgiveness of their sins.

Because of God's tender mercy,

the morning light from heaven is about to break upon us,

to give light to those who sit in darkness and in the shadow of death,

and to guide us to the path of peace." (Luke 1:67–79, NLT)

Meditation

What an amazing passage! When Zechariah and Elizabeth have a son, he prophesies that baby's mission. It so clearly states who and what Jesus Christ will do for Israel and for the entire world, and how John will fit into the incredible redemption that will cause "the morning light from heaven to . . . break upon us." And that happens because of "God's tender mercy."

I recall an instance when, as a child, I was rude and obnoxious to my mother. Usually that would have meant swift and immediate discipline, but that day my mother reacted in a way that caused me to be much more repentant than if she'd carried out her typical punishment. She simply responded gently and kindly, making me thoroughly ashamed of my behavior. I immediately changed my tune, as I wanted to respond to the tenderness she was showing me.

This is a very poor illustration of God's tenderness toward us. How many times do we ignore, defy, or respond ungratefully to God? If you are like me, it's more than you can possibly count. Yet God shows me tender mercy. That means that when I am afraid, he is safe. He is tender and will care for me no matter what life throws at me. As it says in Zephaniah 3:17 (NLT):

With his love, he will calm all your fears.

He will rejoice over you with joyful songs.

Today, as you encounter things that make you anxious, let the knowledge of "God's tender mercy" fill you with peace.

Prayer

Heavenly Father, I am grateful beyond words that you deal tenderly with me. I need your kindness and gentleness to wrap me in security so that I can trust you with every difficult thing in my life. Help me to remember that today, and to be confident I have a safe place to land in your tenderness.

P.M. Meditation

Did you keep in mind that God is full of tenderness toward you? If not, what is keeping you from that knowledge and understanding? Spend some time sorting through what has given you a false view of God, and rest in the truth that he is kinder and gentler than you could ever imagine.

Day 35: Who Is God?

Heavenly

A.M. Meditation

Scripture Passage

I trust in the Lord for protection.

So why do you say to me,

  "Fly like a bird to the mountains for safety!

The wicked are stringing their bows

  and fitting their arrows on the bowstrings.

They shoot from the shadows

  at those whose hearts are right.

The foundations of law and order have collapsed.

  What can the righteous do?"

But the Lord is in his holy Temple;

the Lord still rules from heaven.

He watches everyone closely,

examining every person on earth.

The Lord examines both the righteous and the wicked.

He hates those who love violence.

He will rain down blazing coals and burning sulfur on the wicked,

punishing them with scorching winds.

For the righteous Lord loves justice.

The virtuous will see his face. (Ps. 11, NLT)

Meditation

As we've said before, God is entirely different from us. And one way this is true is that he rules from heaven. From his vantage point, he sees things we cannot see and understands what we cannot grasp. His view (and control) of what is happening is complete; our knowledge is stinted and small. This passage helps us gain a glimpse of the totality of God's knowledge.

Psalm 11 begins with total chaos. Little has changed in 3,000 years. God alone is our protection, because we cannot count on human institutions. They will always disappoint us. And for many in the world, simply being made righteous in Christ is enough to put a target on their backs.

So what can the righteous do? We can know that "the Lord is in his holy Temple; the Lord still rules from heaven." The certainty that he is a heavenly being who is above the fray is enough to give us peace and confidence. He will judge those who love wickedness, and the "virtuous will see his face." Or, as *The Message* puts it:

> God's business is putting things right;
>
> he loves getting the lines straight,
>
> Setting us straight. Once we're standing tall,
>
> we can look him straight in the eye.

This means that when we are frightened and worried, we can run to God for refuge, knowing that with his heavenly perspective, he will bring order to chaos and accomplish his larger plan, of which we are mostly ignorant. Nevertheless, we can trust him and depend on his care for us.

As you face things that make you fear today, let the phrase "the Lord still rules from heaven" take root in your heart to give you confidence that nothing is out of his control or takes him by surprise.

Prayer

Heavenly Father, I am grateful that you never lose perspective. Nothing strikes you unaware, and you alone see the whole picture. Help me to trust you with my little corner of the masterpiece you are weaving and to rest in your wisdom. Thank you that you rule from heaven over all that happens here on earth.

P.M. Meditation

Is it getting easier to recognize your fears and worries when you encounter them? Are you quicker to discover why you are feeling anxious? If so, you are making progress. Recognizing our fears is a large part of the battle. Once we understand what is making us worry we can give it over to our God, who rules from heaven and who will always do the right thing.

Day 36: Who Is God?

Intercessor

A.M. Meditation

Scripture Passage

Meanwhile, the moment we get tired in the waiting, God's Spirit is right alongside helping us along. If we don't know how or what to pray, it doesn't matter. He does our praying in and for us, making prayer out of our wordless sighs, our aching groans. He knows us far better than we know ourselves, knows our pregnant condition, and keeps us present before God. That's why we can be so sure that every detail in our lives of love for God is worked into something good.

God knew what he was doing from the very beginning. He decided from the outset to shape the lives of those who love him along the same lines as the life of his Son. The Son stands first in the line of humanity he restored. We see the original and intended shape of our lives there in him. After God made that decision of what his children should be like, he followed it up by calling people by name. After he called them by name, he set them on a solid basis with himself. And then, after getting them established, he stayed with them to the end, gloriously completing what he had begun. (Rom. 8:26–30, MSG)

Meditation

We cannot forget that God is three-in-one. That means the Holy Spirit is as much God as are the Father and the Son (all three persons of the Trinity are clearly reflected in this passage).

When we trust Christ, God gives us his Spirit so we will never be alone or feel abandoned. He doesn't tell us to gut it out on our own. Instead, he offers himself as a constant guide.

A huge part of his presence is that he prays for us, "making prayer out of our wordless sighs, our aching groans." How comforting! When we are anxious and afraid—maybe so frightened that we can't even form words—the Holy Spirit is turning our sighs and groans into a prayer for exactly what we need.

The verse Christians are most familiar with in this passage is Romans 8:28, which the ESV translates: "And we know that for those who love God all things work together for good, for those who are called according to his purpose." I love the way Eugene Peterson translates it in *The Message*, tying it in to the earlier verses. The reason God is working things together for good is that he knows us intimately, and is even praying for us in the way we need him to so that we can become more like Christ.

What a fantastic thing to know when we are fearful. God himself is praying for us and guiding us in the way that is best for us. That puts everything in perspective, even in the most terrifying scenario.

Keep the phrase "He does our praying in and for us" in mind today as you face those things that make your heart beat faster. Know that he is constantly praying for you and bringing you through to victory.

Prayer

I love that you know my thoughts before I even say them aloud. And if I can't find the words, you even supply those. What a wonderful God you are! I am grateful that you never abandon me but always surround me with your Spirit to guide and care for me. Help me to remember that today.

P.M. Meditation

Did you keep in mind that God is praying for you? Were you able to rest in that with the confidence that you are being carried and cared for? If not, dwell on that now and rest well tonight.

Day 37: Who Is God?

Bountiful

A.M. Meditation

Scripture Passage

Oh, visit the earth,

    ask her to join the dance!

Deck her out in spring showers,

    fill the God-River with living water.

Paint the wheat fields golden.

    Creation was made for this!

Drench the plowed fields,

    soak the dirt clods

With rainfall as harrow and rake

bring her to blossom and fruit.

Snow-crown the peaks with splendor,

scatter rose petals down your paths,

All through the wild meadows, rose petals.

Set the hills to dancing,

Dress the canyon walls with live sheep,

a drape of flax across the valleys.

Let them shout, and shout, and shout!

Oh, oh, let them sing! (Ps. 65:9–13, MSG)

Meditation

Someone asked me recently when I am most aware of God's presence. I didn't even have to think about it, but immediately answered, "When I'm outside." When I behold the vastness of God's creation, I am overwhelmed by its splendor and bounty. I have the best conversations with God when I am looking around at what he has made, and all of my problems are brought into perspective in light of his power and majesty displayed in earth's "dance," mentioned in this psalm.

No matter what is going on in my life circumstantially and materially, seeing spring showers, wheat fields, plowed fields, blossoms, fruit, peaks, rose petals, and sheep (all things mentioned in this psalm) fills me with wonder and a deep sense that God is good and eager to lavish that goodness on me. And that truly makes me want to shout and sing along with all of creation.

So as you go about your day, reflect on the bounty God has given us in his creation. As you do that, start thanking him for all the ways he has blessed you. Ponder the phrase "fill the God-River with living water," and let our bountiful God fill your heart and mind with his river of living water that is far greater than anything in creation.

Prayer

Creator God, I love the world you have made and am in awe of your creative power. As I come across things that make me fearful and anxious today, I pray that you will remind me of what a bountiful, good God you are and that you want to lavish your plenty on me. I pray my fears will flee in the face of that knowledge.

P.M. Meditation

Did you have time to reflect on what a generous, bountiful God we have? If not, take time to do so now. Take a few minutes and jot down all the ways God has been bountiful with you throughout your life. As you lie down to sleep tonight, let those good thoughts float through your mind.

Day 38: Who Is God?

Creator

A.M. Meditation

Scripture Passage

Christ is the visible image of the invisible God.

He existed before anything was created and is supreme over all creation,

for through him God created everything

in the heavenly realms and on earth.

He made the things we can see

and the things we can't see—

such as thrones, kingdoms, rulers, and authorities in the unseen world.

Everything was created through him and for him.

He existed before anything else,

  and he holds all creation together.

Christ is also the head of the church,

  which is his body.

He is the beginning,

  supreme over all who rise from the dead.

  So he is first in everything.

For God in all his fullness

  was pleased to live in Christ,

and through him God reconciled

  everything to himself.

He made peace with everything in heaven and on earth

  by means of Christ's blood on the cross. (Col. 1:15–20, NLT)

Meditation

Thinking about God's bounty in creation made me want to dwell more on that creation. It is almost impossible for me to think about creation without thinking about God. We often think of God the Father as the one who created everything, but Colossians 1 makes it clear that Christ was an integral part of that process.

This passage also expands my idea of creation beyond the confines of earth, since it mentions the heavenly realms and "thrones, kingdoms, rulers, and authorities in the unseen world." Knowing that is important because it reminds us that something is going on far beyond what we can see, which puts our fears in their proper place.

After all, if I fear something that threatens me here on earth, I know I'm seeing only a small part of what God is doing in the bigger picture. There is an entire realm I know nothing about, which he created and where he is working out his plan. And that plan revolves around reconciling everything to himself, making "peace with everything in heaven and on earth." What, then, could I possibly fear?

As you go about your day, keep in mind that God is "supreme over all creation." Let that phrase flow through your heart and mind as your anxiety grows over something in your path. You will surely gain confidence as this truth becomes predominant in your thoughts.

Prayer

Lord, I am grateful that you not only made the earth and the heavenly realms, but are also supreme over it all. Nothing is outside of your purpose and power. The chaos I feel never touches you, because you feel no anxiety about it. Help me to rest in that knowledge and to let your Holy Spirit's confidence flow through me today.

P.M. Meditation

How did you treat the anxieties and fears that came your way today? Were you able to remember that God is supreme over whatever is worrying you? If not, give him those worries now, and trust that he is big and wise enough to handle them perfectly. After all, he set the entire universe into motion, and none of it escapes his care and notice.

Day 39: Who Is God?

Generous

A.M. Meditation

Scripture Passage

Once Jesus was in a certain place praying. As he finished, one of his disciples came to him and said, "Lord, teach us to pray, just as John taught his disciples."

Jesus said, "This is how you should pray:

"Father, may your name be kept holy.

May your Kingdom come soon.

Give us each day the food we need,

and forgive us our sins,

as we forgive those who sin against us.

And don't let us yield to temptation."

Then, teaching them more about prayer, he used this story: "Suppose you went to a friend's house at midnight, wanting to borrow three loaves of bread. You say to him, 'A friend of mine has just arrived for a visit, and I have nothing for him to eat.' And suppose he calls out from his bedroom, 'Don't bother me. The door is locked for the night, and my family and I are all in bed. I can't help you.' But I tell you this— though he won't do it for friendship's sake, if you keep knocking long enough, he will get up and give you whatever you need because of your shameless persistence.

"And so I tell you, keep on asking, and you will receive what you ask for. Keep on seeking, and you will find. Keep on knocking, and the door will be opened to you. For everyone who asks, receives. Everyone who seeks, finds. And to everyone who knocks, the door will be opened.

"You fathers—if your children ask for a fish, do you give them a snake instead? Or if they ask for an egg, do you give them a scorpion? Of course not! So if you sinful people know how to give good gifts to your children, how much more will your heavenly Father give the Holy Spirit to those who ask him." (Luke 11:9–13, NLT)

Meditation

Luke 11 begins with Jesus' disciples asking him to teach them to pray. To do that, he gives them the model we commonly call the "Lord's Prayer." Jesus then immediately tells a very human story about someone who gives another person what they ask for merely because of their audacity or persistence (depending on the translation you use). He then tells us to ask, seek, and knock, and contrasts the previous story of someone who gives out of annoyance with the fact that our Father God is far more generous than any human, even a devoted parent.

Finally, he focuses on how our heavenly Father gives us the Holy Spirit—one who will be with us every moment of the day, will always be aware of our needs, and is more generous than anyone we know on earth. We ask him for bread, and he gives us bread, but he also gives us himself. Wow!

So what does that have to do with fear? We are never abandoned. We are always in God's company through his Spirit, and because of that he is always aware of our needs. He will care and provide for us as we trust him with the details of our lives.

As you go about your day, keep the phrase "Lord, teach me to pray" in mind. Ask him to guide you in your ability to communicate with him at all times. Also, ask him to teach you how to let him lead in all the details of your day, especially those that cause you fear and anxiety. Rest in the fact that he is a generous God.

Prayer

Heavenly Father, thank you for giving me your Holy Spirit, who will be with me every moment and who will lavish your generosity on me in ways I can't even imagine. Give me a heart of gratitude, and confidence in your desire to care for me, especially when I am facing something I often worry about.

P.M. Meditation

Hopefully, you were able to trust God's generosity toward you today when you encountered things that caused you worry, anxiety, or fear. If not, ponder all the ways God has been generous to you in the past, and trust his generosity for your future.

Day 40: Who Is God?

Perfect

A.M. Meditation

Scripture Passage

"To the faithful you show yourself faithful;

to those with integrity you show integrity.

To the pure you show yourself pure,

but to the crooked you show yourself shrewd.

You rescue the humble,

but your eyes watch the proud and humiliate them.

O Lord, you are my lamp.

The Lord lights up my darkness.

In your strength I can crush an army;

with my God I can scale any wall.

God's way is perfect.

All the Lord's promises prove true.

He is a shield for all who look to him for protection.

For who is God except the Lord?

Who but our God is a solid rock?

God is my strong fortress,

and he makes my way perfect." (2 Sam. 22:26–33, ESV)

Meditation

This passage is an excerpt from a song David sang to the Lord on the day God rescued him from Saul and other enemies. I love that about David—after a harrowing day, he takes time to compose a song of praise to God. I want to learn from his example.

Anyway, David begins this song by observing that God reveals himself through our filters. Those who are faithful, have integrity, and are pure can identify those qualities in God.

If, however, the person is crooked (or not faithful, doesn't have integrity, and isn't pure), God shows himself shrewd and humiliates the proud. He lights the darkness and gives strength to the humble. David concludes the song with confidence that God's way is perfect and that all his promises prove true.

What does that mean for our fears? David states clearly in this passage that God is a shield for those who look to him for protection. He is our solid rock, our fortress. And he concludes with "he makes my way perfect." That doesn't mean everything will always be hunky dory in our eyes, but it does mean that he is using whatever circumstances come our way to mold us and make us faithful, pure, and filled with integrity. Because he is perfect, he is continually perfecting us. So what could we possibly fear?

As you go through your day, keep in mind that "God's way is perfect." Let that knowledge fill you with peace no matter what you face.

Prayer

I am grateful, Lord, that you don't leave me stuck in my crookedness and imperfections, but instead are constantly shaping me in your image. I know I will never be perfect as you are, but I am so glad you never give up on me as you move me away from my fears and anxieties into your perfection.

P.M. Meditation

Were you able to keep in mind that a perfect God has perfect promises and perfect ways? If not, spend time dwelling once again on David's prayer in 2 Samuel 22:26–33, and rest well in the knowledge of his complete inability to do anything wrong.

Final Thoughts

I hope dwelling on who God is for 40 days has helped you move past your fears and rest in his love and goodness. My prayer for you is that you will never go back to being as frightened and anxious as you were before taking this time to undo any faulty ideas you had about God and replacing them with the truth: that you are cared for by the Creator of the universe who will never leave you or abandon you.

If you found help through this book, pass it on to others who may need it. Also, I offer an abbreviated version of the contents of this book in a **weekend retreat** format. If your church or parachurch group would be interested in hosting such a retreat, go to johannahreardon.com to find out more.

About the Author

Besides this book, JoHannah Reardon has written a family devotional and many novels. Check out all her books and follow her blog at johannahreardon.com; on Facebook at JoHannah Reardon—freelance writer; on Twitter at @johannahreardon; and on Pinterest.

Family Devotional: *Proverbs for Kids*

Devotionals: *No More Fear, Undone by Majesty and Mystery*

Blackberry County Chronicles: *Crispens Point—Book 1, Cherry Cobbler—Book 2, Prince Crossing—Book 3*

Distant Shores Series: *Redbud Corner—Book 1, Highland Path—Book 2, Gathering Bittersweet—Book 3*

Fairy Tale: The Land of Neo Trilogy

Made in the USA
Monee, IL
09 September 2020